STRATEGIES for Writers
Practice the Strategy
Notebook

Level E

Authors

Leslie W. Crawford, Ed.D.
Georgia College & State University

Rebecca Bowers Sipe, Ed.D.
Eastern Michigan University

Cover Design
Tommaso Design Group

Production by Laurel Tech Integrated Publishing Services

ISBN 0-7367-1247-X

Zaner-Bloser, Inc., P.O. Box 16764, Columbus, Ohio 43216-6764   (1-800-421-3018)

Printed in the United States of America

   03   04   05   06   MZ   5   4   3   2

NARRATIVE
writing

DESCRIPTIVE
writing

Table of Contents

EXPOSITORY
writing

NARRATIVE
writing

PERSUASIVE

writing

TEST

writing

Prewriting

Gather

Look at photographs to get ideas. Pick a photo that reminds me of a personal experience.

your own writing

Now it's your turn to practice this strategy with a different topic. Look at the pictures on this page. Think about fun places you have been. What story could you tell? (Remember, this is a personal narrative. The story must be about you.) Circle the photo that reminds you—at least a little—of an experience you have had.

Prewriting

Gather

Look at photographs to get ideas. Pick a photo that reminds me of a personal experience.

Use this page to gather more ideas for your personal narrative. Explain your reasons for selecting the photo you circled on the previous page. Why could this personal experience make a good story?

_____

_____

_____

_____

_____

_____

_____

_____

_____

_____

_____

_____

_____

_____

 Now go back to Janell's work on page 21 in the Student Edition.

Use after page 21 in the Student Edition.

Prewriting

Organize

Organize my thoughts in a storyboard.

your own writing

Now it's time for you to practice this strategy. Use the four circles on this page to draw pictures to create a storyboard. The storyboard should show the events in the body of your narrative.

Event 1

Event 2

Event 3

Event 4

 Now go back to Janell's work on page 22 in the Student Edition.

Narrative Writing • Personal Narrative

DRafting

Write

Draft the body of my personal narrative by writing one or more sentences about each picture on my storyboard.

your own writing

Now it's time for you to practice this strategy. Study the storyboard pictures you created on page 8. On this page, write at least two sentences that tell what is happening in each picture. Then, reread your description of the events that will make up the body of your story.

Event 1

_____
_____
_____
_____
_____
_____

Event 2

_____
_____
_____
_____
_____
_____

Event 3

_____
_____
_____
_____
_____
_____

Event 4

_____
_____
_____
_____
_____
_____

RETURN Now go back to Janell's work on page 24 in the Student Edition.

ReVising

Elaborate
Write an introduction and a conclusion that will interest my reader.

Remember the picture of the roller coaster on page 6? One student writer chose to write about a roller coaster ride. Here is this writer's introduction. Read the introduction and then rewrite it to make it better. Remember, a good introduction grabs the reader's attention.

> I was happy because we were going to the amusement park. I wanted to ride the **Apollo** for the first time. I couldn't wait. I told my friends about it.

_____

_____

_____

_____

_____

Now read and rewrite this writer's conclusion. Make it better, too. A good conclusion ties up loose ends, provides a good summary, and leaves the reader satisfied.

> I was disappointed. I couldn't ride the **Apollo** roller coaster because I was too short. My brother and I rode the **Junior Apollo.** It made me feel a little better.

_____

_____

_____

_____

_____

_____

ReVising

Elaborate

Write an introduction and a conclusion that will interest my reader.

your own writing

Now it's time for you to practice this strategy. On the following lines, write a good introduction and a good conclusion for your own personal narrative about your experience.

My Introduction

_____

_____

_____

_____

_____

_____

My Conclusion

_____

_____

_____

_____

_____

_____

 Now go back to Janell's work on page 26 in the Student Edition.

Narrative Writing • Personal Narrative

ReVising

Clarify

Replace overused words and clichés with more exact words and fresh language.

Now it's time for you to practice this strategy. Revise this draft of a personal narrative about a roller coaster ride. Delete or replace the underlined words with words that are more exact and fresh. Correct any other errors you find, too.

I thought we would never get to the front of the line <u>in a million years</u>! Every time a coaster roared by us, I got <u>really</u> excited. Finally, it was our turn. As I started through the gate, a gigantic hand <u>came out of nowhere and held</u> me back. "Say there, young lady," a loud voice <u>said</u>. "I believe that your a bit to short to ride the **Apollo**."

<u>I couldn't believe my ears</u>! I stood beside the <u>really</u> colorful sign that showed how tall riders had to be. My family sighed and shook their heads. "You're an inch too short," they <u>said</u> <u>really</u> sadly. My older brother put his arm around my shoulders and <u>said</u>, "Follow me. I have a <u>really</u> good idea!" The rest of our family got on the **Apollo**. My brother led me through the park. I followed behind him <u>as slow as a turtle</u> until I saw another roller coaster, the **Junior Apollo**.

Copyright © Zaner-Bloser, Inc.

 Now go back to Janell's work on page 28 in the Student Edition.

Editing

Proofread Make sure I have avoided run-on sentences by joining compound sentences correctly.

⌐ Indent.
≡ Make a capital.
╱ Make a small letter.
∧ Add something.
ℓ Take out something.
⊙ Add a period.
⌗ New paragraph
(SP) Spelling error

Now it's time for you to practice this strategy. Here is part of the revised draft of the story about the roller coaster. Use the proofreading marks to correct any errors. Use a dictionary to help with spelling.

I couldn't believe we were finally on our way to the amusement park! I was six years old and I had been waiting for this trip for a long time. This park had fourteen sensational roller coasters, that was more than any other amusement park in the entire world! I had counted down the weeks, the days, the hours, and the minutes! I rode up and down roller coasters in my dreams at night. My friends at school got tired of hearing about the park but I didn't get tired of talking about it.

My Goal was to ride the **Apollo**. It had two tracks with two trains; and they raced each other! this roller coaster was almost 4,000 feet tall and it went 60 miles per hour, which is unbelieveably fast. When we got to the park, my family had a hard time holding me back. We soon located the **Apollo** on the map and set off to find it. Suddenly I shreeked, "Look! There's the **Apollo**!" I ran as fast as I could and I got in line. It took a while for my parents to catch up with me

I thought we would never get to the front of the line! Every time a coaster roared by us, I got excited. Finally, it was our turn. I started through the gate, and a gigantic hand reached out to hold me back. "Say there, young lady," a loud voice bellowed. "I believe that you're a bit too short to ride the **Apollo**."

Remember:
Use this strategy in
your own
writing

 Now go back to Janell's work on page 30 in the Student Edition.

Narrative Writing • Personal Narrative

Using a Rubric

Use this rubric to evaluate Janell's story on pages 31–33 in your Student Edition. You may work with a partner.

Audience

Does the writer capture and keep the readers' interest?

Organization

How well is the story organized?

Elaboration

Do the introduction and the conclusion add to the narrative?

Clarification

Does the writer choose words that are exact and fresh instead of overused words and clichés?

Conventions & Skills

Are all compound sentences joined correctly?

your own writing

Save this rubric. Use it to check your own writing.

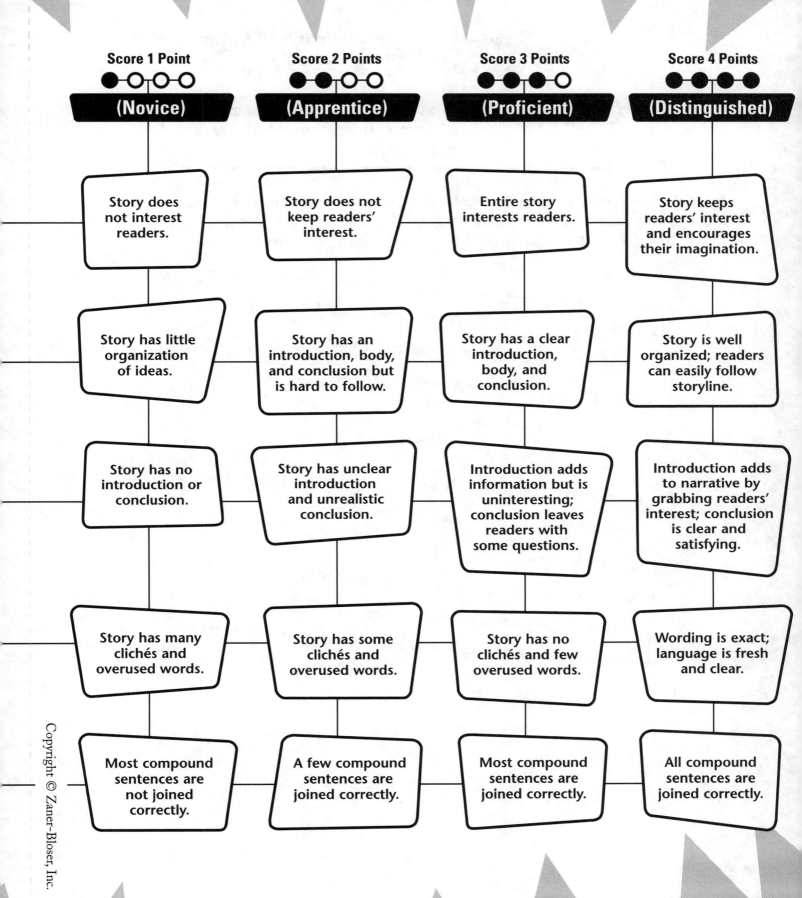

Score 1 Point
● ○ ● ○
(Novice)

Score 2 Points
● ● ○ ○
(Apprentice)

Score 3 Points
● ● ● ○
(Proficient)

Score 4 Points
● ● ● ●
(Distinguished)

Novice	Apprentice	Proficient	Distinguished
Story does not interest readers.	Story does not keep readers' interest.	Entire story interests readers.	Story keeps readers' interest and encourages their imagination.
Story has little organization of ideas.	Story has an introduction, body, and conclusion but is hard to follow.	Story has a clear introduction, body, and conclusion.	Story is well organized; readers can easily follow storyline.
Story has no introduction or conclusion.	Story has unclear introduction and unrealistic conclusion.	Introduction adds information but is uninteresting; conclusion leaves readers with some questions.	Introduction adds to narrative by grabbing readers' interest; conclusion is clear and satisfying.
Story has many clichés and overused words.	Story has some clichés and overused words.	Story has no clichés and few overused words.	Wording is exact; language is fresh and clear.
Most compound sentences are not joined correctly.	A few compound sentences are joined correctly.	Most compound sentences are joined correctly.	All compound sentences are joined correctly.

Prewriting

Gather

Draw on my memory of an incident. Jot down what I saw and heard.

Now it's your turn to practice this strategy with a different topic. Read the following memories about watching a shuttle launch at the Kennedy Space Center. A writer might include these memories in an eyewitness account.

- feeling excitement in the crowd before blast-off
- watching huge clouds of smoke and steam
- seeing flames coming out of the rockets
- feeling the earth shake
- hearing a huge roar
- watching all the birds fly away
- cheering as Discovery rose into the sky
- counting down to blast-off
- wondering if the launch would be postponed
- finding marshes close to the space center

PrewRiting

Gather

Draw on my memory of an incident. Jot down what I saw and heard.

your own writing

Now think of an incident that you remember. Jot down what you saw and heard during the incident.

_____

_____

_____

_____

_____

_____

_____

_____

_____

_____

_____

_____

_____

_____

_____

_____

_____

RETURN Now go back to William's work on page 45 in the Student Edition.

PReWRitiNg

Organize Make a sequence chain of the most important events.

Here's how one writer filled in the sequence chain of an eyewitness account of the shuttle launch.

Topic:	Shuttle launch

First Event:	driving to the space center

Next Event:	feeling excitement in the crowd at the site

Next Event:	counting down to the blast-off

Next Event:	seeing the flames and feeling the rumble

Final Event:	cheering as Discovery rose into the sky

PreWriting

Organize Make a sequence chain of the most important events.

your own writing

Now it's time for you to practice this strategy. Think about the important events in the incident you selected. Make a sequence chain that shows the events in the order they happened. You can add more event boxes to your sequence chain if you need them.

Topic:

First Event:

↓

Next Event:

↓

Next Event:

↓

Next Event:

↓

Final Event:

RETURN Now go back to William's work on page 46 in the Student Edition.

Drafting

Write

Draft my account by writing one paragraph for every part of my sequence chain.

your own writing

Now it's time for you to practice this strategy. Reread the events you identified on page 19. Use the boxes on this page and the next page to write a paragraph for every event on your sequence chain.

Topic:

First Event:

Next Event:

Drafting

Write

Draft my account by writing one paragraph for every part of my sequence chain.

Next Event:

Next Event:

Final Event:

Now go back to William's work on page 48 in the Student Edition.

Narrative Writing • Eyewitness Account

ReVising

Elaborate
Add quotes to make my account more interesting.

Now it's time for you to practice this strategy. Read this section of an eyewitness account about a shuttle launch. Notice that it has no quotes. Imagine some interesting things that the people in this account might have said. Write in your quotes. (In a real eyewitness account, of course, you would not make up quotes. You would write down what the people actually say!)

Suddenly a cheer rose. "_____

_____!" the crowd yelled. People

waved flags and chanted, "_____

_____" Strangers hugged each

other and exchanged high-fives. A man standing next to me said,

"_____

_____"

My mom and I grinned and jumped up and down. My father wiped a

tear from his eye. "_____

_____,"

he mumbled. He continued to watch the sky long after the shuttle and its

long trail of smoke had disappeared. I gave him a hug and said,

"_____

_____

_____."

 Now go back to William's work on page **49** in the Student Edition.

Remember: Use this strategy in **your own writing**

22 **Narrative Writing** • Eyewitness Account

ReVising

Clarify

Make sure the order of sentences in each paragraph is logical.

Now it's time for you to practice this strategy. Read this section from a draft about the shuttle launch. Two of the sentences are out of order. Can you find them? Draw a circle around each sentence and use an arrow to show where it belongs. Then rewrite the paragraph so that the sentence order is more logical.

We arrived there early in the morning, just as the sun was beginning to rise. We saw blue herons, brown pelicans, storks, and terns. As we drove closer to the space center, we passed marshes and ponds. They looked peaceful and quiet, not at all what I had expected. Then in the distance, we saw discovery sitting on the launch pad. "I'll bet those birds won't be so peaceful a few hours from now," my father remarked. Kennedy Space Center is located just off the east coast of Florida on Merritt Island, and it is a beautiful sight.

_____

_____

_____

_____

_____

_____

_____

_____

Remember: Use this strategy in **your own writing**

 RETURN Now go back to William's work on page 50 in the Student Edition.

⌐ Indent.	ℓ Take out something.
≡ Make a capital.	⊙ Add a period.
/ Make a small letter.	⌗ New paragraph
∧ Add something.	ⓢⓟ Spelling error

Editing

Proofread

Check for the correct forms of all pronouns.

Now it's time for you to practice this strategy. Here is the revised draft of the eyewitness account of the shuttle launch. Use the proofreading marks to correct any errors. Use a dictionary to help with spelling.

A Special Discovery

I and my family drove for two days to get to Kennedy Space Center. The shuttle Discovery was scheduled to blast off on March 8 at 10:00 in the morning, and we were determined to see it. We knew that mechanical problems or bad weather could postpone the launch, so we kept our fingers crossed the entire way to Florida.

Kennedy Space Center is located just off the east coast of Florida on Merritt Island, and it is a beautiful sight. We arrived there early in the morning, just as the sun was beginning to rise. I had seen the island on television many times, but I just couldn't believe my family and me were really there. As we drove closer to the space center, we passed marshes and ponds. We saw blue herons, brown pelicans, storks, and terns. They looked peaceful and quiet, not at all what I had expected. Then in the distance, we saw discovery sitting on the launch pad. "I'll bet those birds won't be so peaceful a few hours from now, my father remarked. When we got to the viewing site, it was like a carnival. Hundreds of people were already there, talking and laughing. Cameras and binoculars were everywhere. All the people kept his eyes on Discovery, even tho it wasn't scheduled to blast off right away. I ran ahead and found a

⌐ Indent.

≡ Make a capital.

／ Make a small letter.

∧ Add something.

℘ Take out something.

⊙ Add a period.

New paragraph

SP Spelling error

Editing

Proofread

Check for the correct forms of all pronouns.

place for we. We'll be able to see everything from here," I said excitedly. We unpacked food, sunglasses, sunscreen, our camera, and a blanket and settled in to enjoy the launch. I saw a man who looked just like my teacher down there.

Time past, but not quickly enough for me. When the countdown finally began, Dad and me joined in. "Ten, nine, eight, seven, six, five, four, three, two, one!" the crowd chanted. Tension filled the air.

What happened next is hard to describe. Huge clouds of smoke and steam billowed down onto the lunch pad. Then bright orange rocket flames appeared, and Discovery slowly began to rise. The earth gave a mighty rumble and began to shake, and the loudest noise I have ever heard filled the air. Birds filled the air, too, as the shuttle rose higher and higher. No one move. No one spoke. We all just stood there taking in the Awesome Sight.

Suddenly a cheer rose. "Hurray! Look at her go! She's on her way!" the crowd yelled. People waved flags and chanted, "USA! USA! USA!" Strangers hugged each other and exchanged high-fives.

Mom and me grinned and jumped up and down. My father wiped a tear from his eye. "Have a safe trip, he mumbled. He continued to watch the sky long after the shuttle and it's long trail of smoke had disappeared. I gave him a hug and said, Thanks for bringing us here, Dad."

Remember: Use this strategy in **your own writing**

Now go back to William's work on page 52 in the Student Edition.

Using a Rubric

Use this rubric to score William's story on pages 53–55 in your Student Edition. You may work with a partner.

Audience

How well does the writer capture and hold the reader's interest?

Organization

Are the events presented in the order they happened?

Elaboration

Does the writer use quotes to make the account more interesting?

Clarification

Are the sentences in the most logical order?

your own writing

Save this rubric. Use it to check your own writing.

Conventions & Skills

Does the writer use the correct forms of all pronouns?

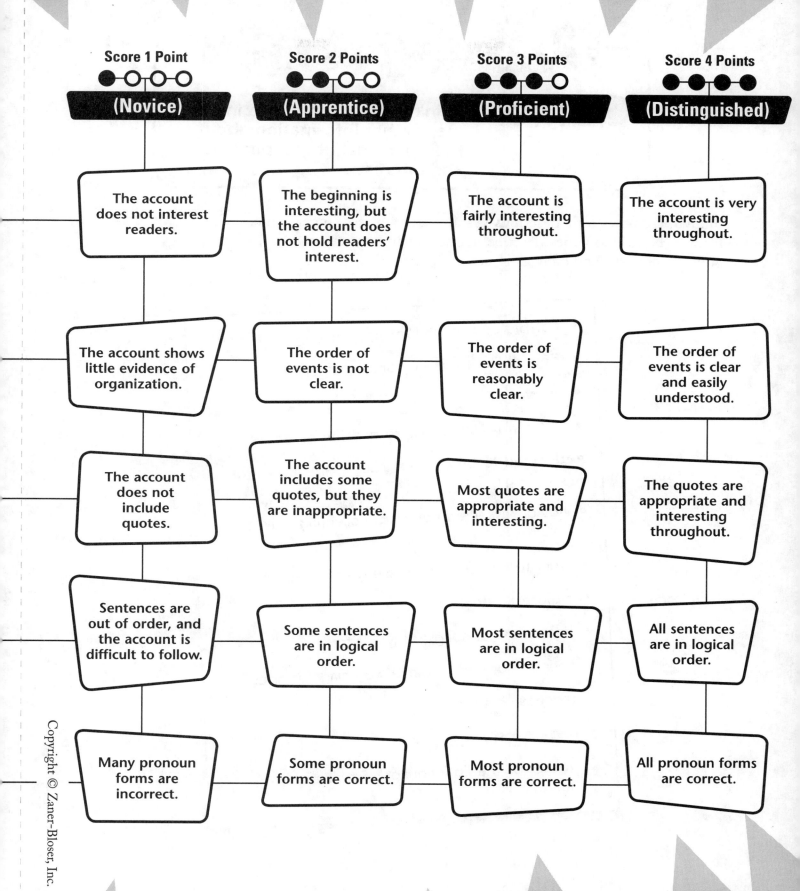

Score 1 Point (Novice)

- The account does not interest readers.
- The account shows little evidence of organization.
- The account does not include quotes.
- Sentences are out of order, and the account is difficult to follow.
- Many pronoun forms are incorrect.

Score 2 Points (Apprentice)

- The beginning is interesting, but the account does not hold readers' interest.
- The order of events is not clear.
- The account includes some quotes, but they are inappropriate.
- Some sentences are in logical order.
- Some pronoun forms are correct.

Score 3 Points (Proficient)

- The account is fairly interesting throughout.
- The order of events is reasonably clear.
- Most quotes are appropriate and interesting.
- Most sentences are in logical order.
- Most pronoun forms are correct.

Score 4 Points (Distinguished)

- The account is very interesting throughout.
- The order of events is clear and easily understood.
- The quotes are appropriate and interesting throughout.
- All sentences are in logical order.
- All pronoun forms are correct.

Prewriting

Gather

Think about people who interest me. Gather information about their personalities, appearance, and interests.

Study these notes for a descriptive essay about a forest ranger named Nadine. Notice how they describe her personality, appearance, background, interests, and daily activities.

- not big and tough looking, but very strong

- doesn't "look" like a forest ranger

- not very tall

- has always loved nature and the outdoors

- decided to be a forest ranger when she was a little girl

- has always liked camping, collecting leaves, wildlife

- went to college to become a forest ranger

- majored in forestry

- knows lots of songs; plays guitar

- spends many hours alone watching for fires

- teaches campfire safety

- rescues lost hikers

- works for the National Park Service in Montana

PreWRiTiNg

Gather

Think about people who interest me. Gather information about their personalities, appearance, and interests.

your own writing

Now it's time for you to practice this strategy. Choose someone to write about in a descriptive essay. Use this page for your notes. Your goal is to make your readers feel as if they know this person. Be sure to include details about the person's personality, appearance, interests, achievements, and perhaps daily activities or job responsibilities.

_____
_____
_____
_____
_____
_____
_____
_____
_____
_____
_____
_____
_____
_____
_____
_____
_____

RETURN Now go back to Joseph's work on page 69 in the Student Edition.

PreWRiTinG

Organize

Use my notes to make a spider map.

This is how another writer organized the notes on page 28 into a spider map. Notice how the notes are in categories.

appearance
- not big or tough looking, but very strong
- doesn't look like a forest ranger
- not very tall

personality and interests
- has always loved nature and the outdoors
- has always like camping, collecting leaves, wildlife
- knows lots of songs; plays the guitar
- decided to be a forest ranger when she was a little girl

Nadine, the Forest Ranger

daily activities
- spends many hours alone watching for fires
- teaches campfire safety
- rescues lost hikers

achievements
- works for the National Park Service in Montana
- went to college to become a forest ranger
- majored in forestry

PreWRITINg
Organize
Use my notes to make a spider map.

your own writing

Now it's time for you to practice this strategy. Use the spider map on this page to organize your notes. Write your topic in the circle. Then write details in each category on the lines that extend from the legs.

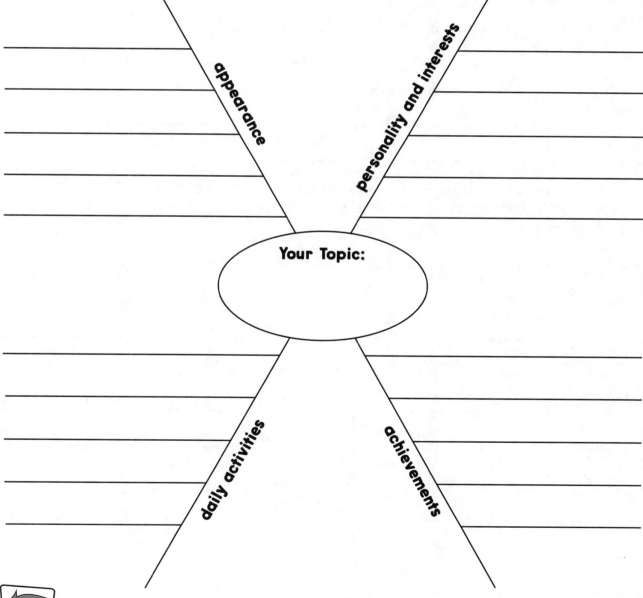

appearance

personality and interests

Your Topic:

daily activities

achievements

RETURN Now go back to Joseph's work on page 70 in the Student Edition.

Drafting

Write

Draft my description. Begin by describing the most interesting thing about my topic.

your own writing

Now it's time for you to practice this strategy. On this page, you are going to write a draft of the first paragraph of your descriptive essay. Study the spider map you made on the last page.

What is the most interesting thing about the person you chose?

_____

Why is this piece of information interesting?

_____

_____

Now draft the first paragraph of your descriptive essay. Be sure to include the interesting thing you chose. Continue writing your essay on the next page.

_____

_____

_____

_____

_____

_____

_____

_____

_____

_____

Descriptive Writing • Descriptive Essay

Drafting

Write

Draft my description. Begin by describing the most interesting thing about my topic.

On this page, you can continue writing your draft of your descriptive essay. Do not forget to refer to the spider map you made.

_____

_____

_____

_____

_____

_____

_____

_____

_____

_____

_____

_____

_____

_____

_____

_____

_____

 Now go back to Joseph's work on page 72 in the Student Edition.

Revising

Elaborate
Add similes to make my description clearer.

Remember that a simile must compare two different things.

> **Not a simile:** You look as tired as I am. (compares two similar things: two people)

> **Simile:** You look as tired as my dog after he runs for a mile. (compares two different things: a person and a dog)

Now it's time for you to practice this strategy. First, underline the three similes below. Identify the two things that are being compared in each simile.

Nadine is a good musician. She named her guitar "Woody," and she treats it like a favorite old friend. Nadine's weathered fingers dance across the strings as delicately as a butterfly, and wonderful music fills the air. Nadine loves to sing, and her voice is as high and clear as a bird's song.

Now decide which of the sentences below contains a simile. Rewrite the two sentences that are not similes, making them into "real" similes.

1. We ran as fast as we could.

_____

2. His head was nodding like a sunflower in a slight breeze.

_____

3. The smell was like nothing I ever smelled before.

_____

Remember: Use this strategy in **your own writing**

RETURN Now go back to Joseph's work on page 73 in the Student Edition.

ReVising

Clarify   Combine short, choppy sentences.

Now it's time for you to practice this strategy. Read this paragraph from the descriptive essay about Nadine. Did you notice how awkward the short, choppy sentences sounded? Revise the paragraph, combining some of the short sentences so they will be easier to read.

My aunt Nadine decided to become a forest ranger. She was eight years old. She loved nature. She was happiest when she was outdoors. Nadine went camping. She collected leaves. She read about wildlife. Actually, it was her reading that helped her choose her profession. She read a comic book about Smokey the Bear. She knew right away what she wanted to do. Not only would she help prevent forest fires, she would help protect the entire forest! That year she decided to become a forest ranger. She dressed like Smokey the Bear on Halloween. She would have worn the costume every day for the rest of the year. Her mother wouldn't let her.

_____

_____

_____

_____

_____

_____

_____

_____

Remember:
Use this strategy in
your own writing

Now go back to Joseph's work on page 74 in the Student Edition.

Editing

Proofread

⊐ Indent.	ℓ Take out something.
☰ Make a capital.	⊙ Add a period.
/ Make a small letter.	♯ New paragraph
∧ Add something.	SP Spelling error

Check to see that plural nouns and possessive nouns are formed correctly.

Now it's time for you to practice this strategy. Here is the revised draft of the descriptive essay about Nadine. Use the proofreading marks to correct any errors, especially mistakes in forming plural nouns and possessive nouns. Use a dictionary to help with spelling.

Smokey the Bear Grows Up

My aunt Nadine decided to become a forest ranger when she was eight years old. She loved nature, and she was happiest when she was outdoors. Nadine went camping, collected leafs, and read everything she could find about wildlife. Actually, it was her reading that helped her choose her profession. When she read a comic book about Smokey the Bear, she knew right away what she wanted to do. Not only would she help prevent forest fire's, she would help protect the entire forest and the foxs and bears and everything in it! That year she decided to become a forest ranger and dressed like Smokey the Bear on Halloween. She would have worn the costume every day for the rest of the year, but her mother wouldn't let her

Nadine knew that she needed to go to College to become a forest ranger. She studied hard and got good grades in high school. Then she got a scholarship and earned a degree in forestry. During Nadines college years, she missed her camping trips and her long walks in the woods. She new her education was important, though. Her hard work paid off when she got a job as a forest ranger with the National Park Service in montana. Today, Nadine lives and works in the woods. She spends a lot of time

Editing

Proofread

⌐ Indent.
    ℓ Take out something.
≡ Make a capital.
    ⊙ Add a period.
/ Make a small letter.
    ⌗ New paragraph
∧ Add something.
    SP Spelling error

Check to see that plural nouns and possessive nouns are formed correctly.

alone, and she often plays the guitar to pass the time. Nadine is a good musician. She named her guitar "Woody," and she treats it like a favorite old friend. Nadines weathered fingers dance across the strings as delicately as a butterfly, and wonderful music fills the air. Nadine loves to sing, and her voice is as high and clear as a birds song. She seems to know every song ever written.

People often question Nadine about being a forest ranger. They'll say, "You don't look like a forest ranger" or "You're so small! I'd hate to see you come up against a big grizzly bear!" She always has a good reply. Sometimes she says, "I may be small, but I'm as strong as Hercules." Other times, she says, "Don't worry about me. I'm as sturdy as an oak!" Nadine says she never knows what will happen next. It might be a forest fire, mooses that have wandered out of the park, or hikers on cliffes who really need to be rescued. Whatever the problem, Nadine is prepared to help.

Nadine still has her old Smokey the Bear costume. She keeps it in her closet as a reminder of the decicion she made so many years ago. She smiles whenever she sees it. Then she looks at the uniform hanging beside it, her National Park Service uniform. She smiles again, and this time her smile is filled with pride. Nadines childhood dream has turned into her life-long profession, and she is glad it did

Remember:
Use this strategy in
your own
writing

Now go back to Joseph's work on page 76 in the Student Edition.

Using a Rubric

Use this rubric to evaluate Joseph's essay on page 77 in your Student Edition. You may work with a partner.

Audience

Does the writer include details that interest the reader?

Organization

Does the writer begin with the most interesting information about the topic and stay on the topic throughout?

Elaboration

How well does the writer use similes to make the description clearer?

Clarification

Does the writer avoid using short, choppy sentences?

Conventions & Skills

Are all plural nouns and possessive nouns formed correctly?

your own writing

Save this rubric. Use it to check your own writing.

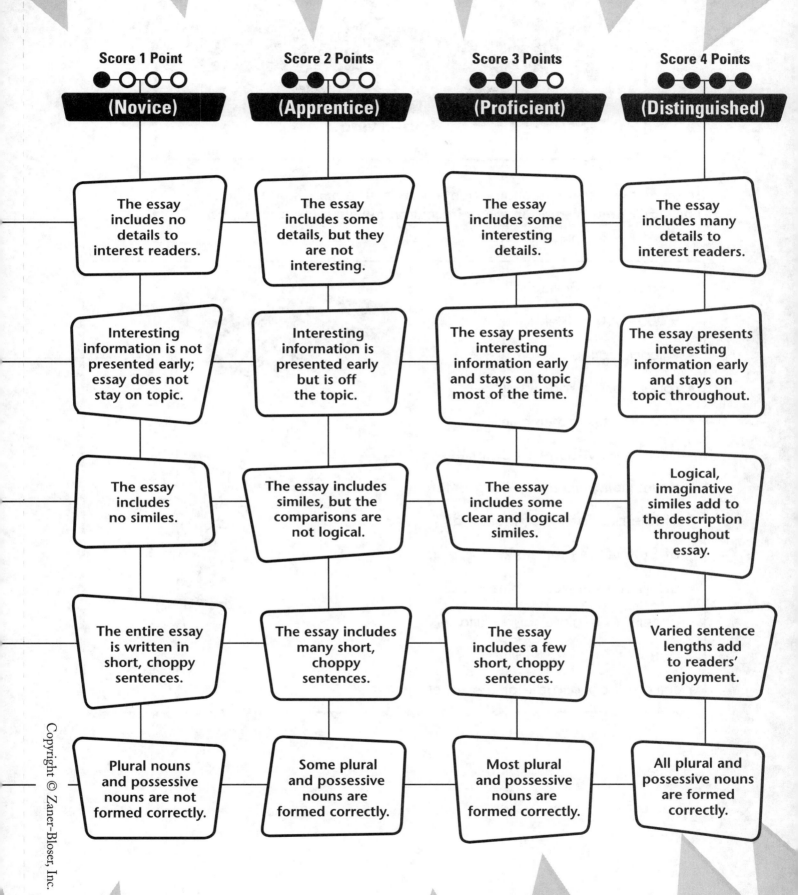

Score 1 Point (Novice)	Score 2 Points (Apprentice)	Score 3 Points (Proficient)	Score 4 Points (Distinguished)
The essay includes no details to interest readers.	The essay includes some details, but they are not interesting.	The essay includes some interesting details.	The essay includes many details to interest readers.
Interesting information is not presented early; essay does not stay on topic.	Interesting information is presented early but is off the topic.	The essay presents interesting information early and stays on topic most of the time.	The essay presents interesting information early and stays on topic throughout.
The essay includes no similes.	The essay includes similes, but the comparisons are not logical.	The essay includes some clear and logical similes.	Logical, imaginative similes add to the description throughout essay.
The entire essay is written in short, choppy sentences.	The essay includes many short, choppy sentences.	The essay includes a few short, choppy sentences.	Varied sentence lengths add to readers' enjoyment.
Plural nouns and possessive nouns are not formed correctly.	Some plural and possessive nouns are formed correctly.	Most plural and possessive nouns are formed correctly.	All plural and possessive nouns are formed correctly.

Prewriting

Gather   Take notes on what I am observing.

Study these notes for an observation report about monarch butterflies.
The writer drew pictures in the right column to help himself remember
details.

- Sierra Madre Mountains

  9,000–12,000 feet

- volcanic range

- forests and meadows

- firs, cypress, other pines

- morning cold, butterflies don't
  move: monarchs try to hang onto
  middle part of trees; thousands
  of butterflies on trees and ground

- afternoon sun warms butterflies:
  butterflies explore, drink, and
  mate

- some fall off and die or get eaten

Prewriting

Gather Take notes on what I am observing.

your own writing

Now it's your turn to practice this strategy. Think about the view outside your classroom window or another window, perhaps at home. Choose something from nature that you would like to observe. Record your notes and make your drawings below. (The drawings should be close-ups.) Your drawings will help you remember important details when you begin to write.

Notes	Drawings

RETURN

Now go back to Rebecca's work on page 87 in the Student Edition.

PreWriting

Organize

Organize my notes into a network tree.

This is how one writer organized the notes on page 40 into a network tree.

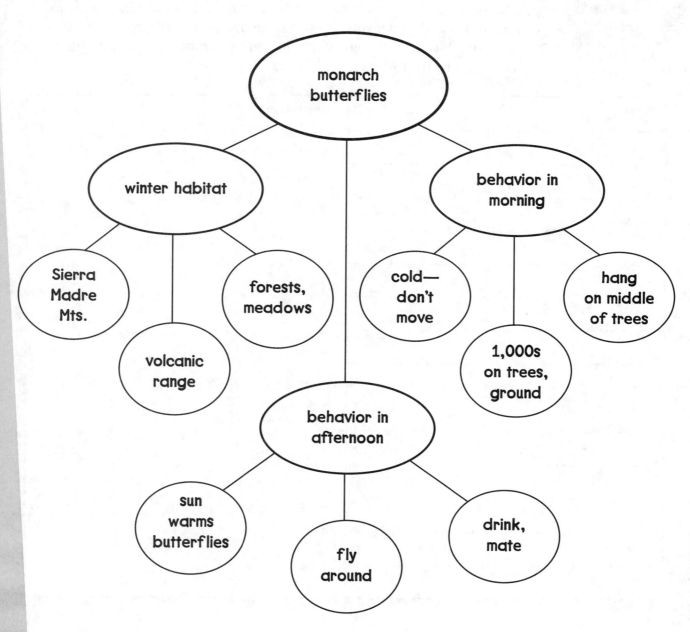

Descriptive Writing • Observation Report

Prewriting

Organize

Organize my notes into a network tree.

your own writing

Now it's time for you to practice this strategy. Use the network tree on this page to organize your notes on page 41. Write your topic at the top. Put your main points at the next level. Then add details about these main points on the bottom level. Add more circles to the middle and bottom levels if you need them.

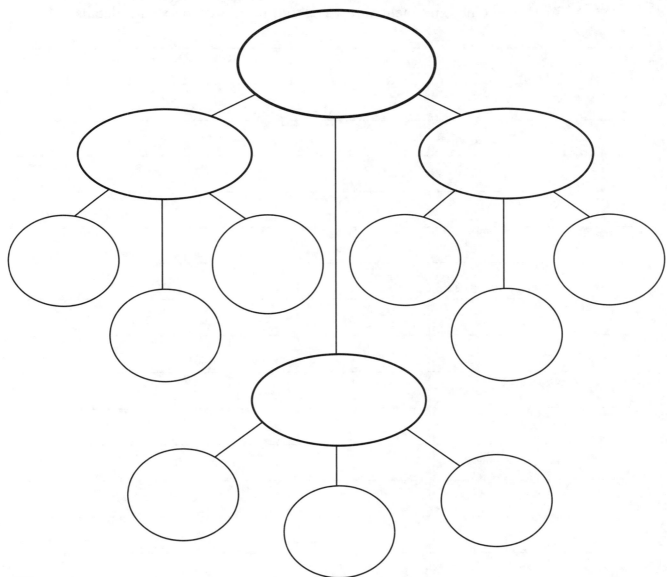

RETURN

Now go back to Rebecca's work on page 88 in the Student Edition.

Drafting

Write

Draft my report. For each main point in my network tree, write a topic sentence and add details.

your own writing

Now it's time for you to practice this strategy. On this page and the next page, you are going to begin writing your observation report. First, review your network tree on page 43. Then start your report below. Remember that each paragraph should begin with a topic sentence and include three or four more sentences with details.

_____

_____

_____

_____

_____

_____

_____

_____

_____

_____

_____

_____

_____

Drafting

Write

Draft my report. For each main point in my network tree, write a topic sentence and add details.

_____

_____

_____

_____

_____

_____

_____

_____

_____

_____

_____

_____

_____

_____

_____

_____

_____

 RETURN Now go back to Rebecca's work on page 90 in the Student Edition.

Revising

Elaborate   Fill in any gaps in my description.

Now it's time for you to practice this strategy. Read this paragraph from an observation report about monarch butterflies. Do any questions come to mind as you read? Do any important details or explanations seem to be missing? You will find more details in the box. Add them to the paragraph wherever you see a gap in the description. Make any other changes necessary to work in the details.

Details

to protect them from the cool temperatures

The forest was mostly firs, cypress trees, and other pines.

They were hanging on trunks and branches and covered the ground like a carpet.

in the Sierra Madre Mountains

We first found the butterflies in the early morning. This forest was cool and still somewhat dark. The forest floor and all the trees seemed to be covered with brown leaves. When we looked closely at these leaves, we realized they were all monarch butterflies. There must have been millions of them! They were absolutely everywhere! The butterflies' wings were tightly closed. Because the butterflies were cold, they did not move.

Remember: Use this strategy in **your own writing**

 Now go back to Rebecca's work on page 91 in the Student Edition.

ReVising

Clarify

Make sure my sentences begin in a variety of ways.

Now it's time for you to practice this strategy. Rewrite the sentences below. Make them more interesting by beginning them with prepositional phrases, other kinds of phrases, and adverbs. Of course, in most of your writing, some of your sentences will begin with the subject.

1. My mother and I drove to the forest early this morning.

_____

2. We had wanted to make this trip for a long time.

_____

3. We finally stopped the car by some thick evergreens.

_____

4. We peered closely at the trees and realized they were covered with butterflies.

_____

5. The air temperature slowly rose.

_____

6. The butterflies became more active in the warmer air.

_____

7. I was fascinated as I watched them begin to open their wings.

_____

8. They soon were ready to fly.

_____

9. They fluttered from tree to tree up and down the mountain slopes.

_____

10. They paused in the sunshine and drank from pools of water.

_____

Remember: Use this strategy in **your own writing**

Now go back to Rebecca's work on page 92 in the Student Edition.

Editing

Proofread

Check to see that all subjects and verbs agree.

⌐ Indent.
≡ Make a capital.
/ Make a small letter.
∧ Add something.
℘ Take out something.
⊙ Add a period.
⌗ New paragraph
ⓢⓟ Spelling error

Now it's time for you to practice this strategy. Here is part of the revised draft of the report about monarch butterflies. Use the proofreading marks to correct any errors. Use a dictionary to help with spelling.

It is early morning. The forest are cool and still somewhat dark. The floor of the forest and all of its trees seems to be covered with brown leaves. When I look at these leaves more closely, I realize that all of them are monarch butterflies. There must be millions of them! They hang on trunks and branches and covers the ground like a carpet. The butterflies' wings are tightly closed to protect them from the lower temperatures. They are cold and does not move.

As the day progresses and the temperature rise, the butterflies become more active. Slowly they opens their wings, and I get a better look at them. Their wings are bright orange with black veins. Each butterfly have too pairs of overlapping wings, a black body speckled with white dots, tow antennae, and six black legs. The butterflies flutter their wings a bit and try to move. When the sun finally warm the forest air, they begin to fly. They flutters from tree to tree as they make their way

Descriptive Writing • Observation Report

Editing

Proofread

Check to see that all subjects and verbs agree.

⌐ Indent.		ℓ	Take out something.
≡ Make a capital.		⊙	Add a period.
/ Make a small letter.		♯	New paragraph
∧ Add something.		㏿	Spelling error

up and down the mountain slopes. Pausing in the sunshine, they drinks from

pools of water. I see pairs of butterflies chase each other through the

air. Their are so many butterflies that I cannot wave my arm without

touching them. At one point, more than a dozen of them lands on me.

    When evening comes, the air grows cool. The monarch butterflies begin

to settle on the trees again. Most attaches themselves around the middle

part of the trees. They seem to realize that they might be picked off by

birds or blown down by the wind if they settles too close to the top. They

also avoid the bottom of the tree trunks and the ground where mice is

scurrying about and looking for food. As the air grow cooler, the butter-

flies close their wings. Some will fall off the trees and onto the ground

during the night. They will be too cold to move, and many will not make

it through the night. Others will cling to the trees until morning, and then

they will begins another day. Soon the butterflies will leave this forest.

I will see some of them again as they passes by my home on their long

journey north.

Remember: Use this strategy in **your own writing**

 Now go back to Rebecca's work on page 94 in the Student Edition.

Using a Rubric

Use this rubric to score Rebecca's story on pages 95–97 in your Student Edition. You may work with a partner.

Audience

Has the writer chosen important details that will inform the reader?

Organization

Are the paragraphs organized with a topic sentence followed by supporting details?

Elaboration

Is the description complete?

Clarification

Do the sentences begin in a variety of ways?

Conventions & Skills

Do all the subjects and verbs agree?

your own writing

Save this rubric. Use it to check your own writing.

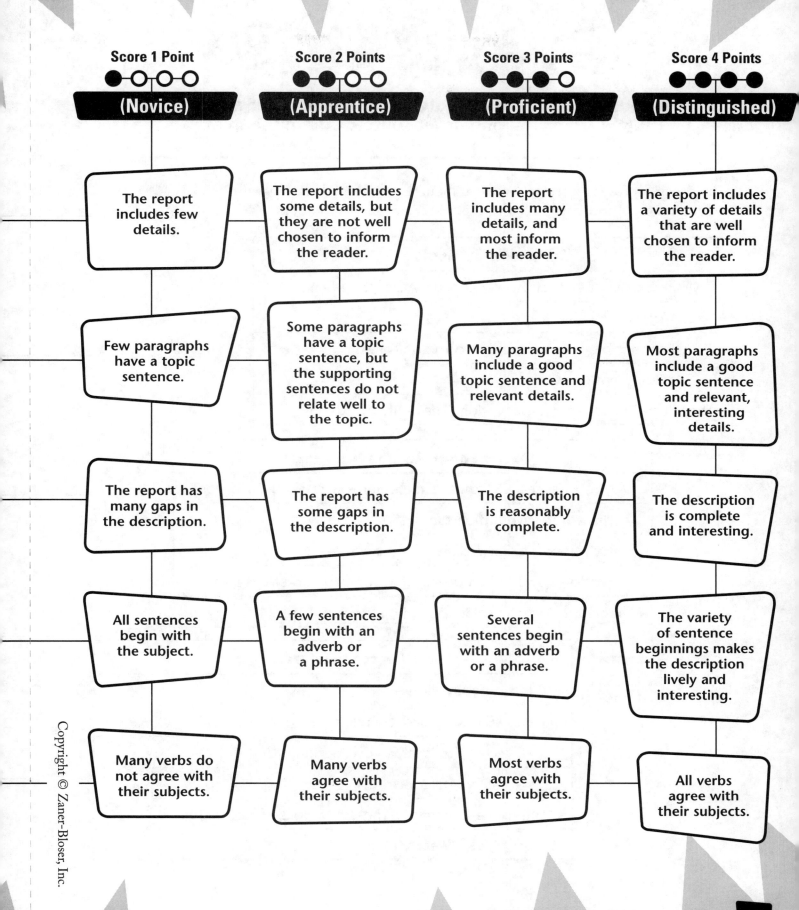

Score 1 Point
● ○ ○ ○
(Novice)

Score 2 Points
● ● ○ ○
(Apprentice)

Score 3 Points
● ● ● ○
(Proficient)

Score 4 Points
● ● ● ●
(Distinguished)

The report includes few details.

The report includes some details, but they are not well chosen to inform the reader.

The report includes many details, and most inform the reader.

The report includes a variety of details that are well chosen to inform the reader.

Few paragraphs have a topic sentence.

Some paragraphs have a topic sentence, but the supporting sentences do not relate well to the topic.

Many paragraphs include a good topic sentence and relevant details.

Most paragraphs include a good topic sentence and relevant, interesting details.

The report has many gaps in the description.

The report has some gaps in the description.

The description is reasonably complete.

The description is complete and interesting.

All sentences begin with the subject.

A few sentences begin with an adverb or a phrase.

Several sentences begin with an adverb or a phrase.

The variety of sentence beginnings makes the description lively and interesting.

Many verbs do not agree with their subjects.

Many verbs agree with their subjects.

Most verbs agree with their subjects.

All verbs agree with their subjects.

PreWRiting

Gather

Take notes from the Internet and at least one other source. Cite my sources.

Study these notes for a research report about Teddy Roosevelt. You will notice that each note card includes the source of the information.

Conservation Goals
Environmental issues that TR worked on while president
1. Water/irrigation
2. Responsible use and preservation of forest
3. Wildlife refuges
Theodore Roosevelt: Conservation President, pp. 61–63

Conservation Accomplishments
• established 18 national monuments (like Grand Canyon)
• created five national parks
• designated 51 wildlife refuges
• added 150 million acres of woods to forest reserves
Theodore Roosevelt: Conservation President, p. 74

Personal Interests
TR led an active life—
• liked hiking and camping
• lived in the West, drove cattle
• went on African safari
"Theodore Roosevelt. The White House Presidential
Biographies" (Web site)

PreWritiNg

Gather

Take notes from the Internet and at least one other source. Cite my sources.

your own writing

Now it's your turn to practice this strategy with a different topic. Select a topic that interests you. Choose another president or world leader. Then choose an Internet site that you believe provides accurate, reliable, up-to-date information. Ask an adult for help, if you wish. Record notes about the person you chose from this Web site and from one other source. You can use the space below or real note cards. Be sure to cite the source of your information.

RETURN Now go back to Selena's work on page 110 in the Student Edition.

PrewRiting
Organize Use my notes to make a support pattern.

The support pattern on the next page was created for a research report on Teddy Roosevelt. It has three main points written on it. Read the facts and notes below and write each one under the appropriate main point on the support pattern on page 55.

Notes

- Environmental issues that TR worked on while President
  1. Water/irrigation
  2. Responsible use and preservation of forest
  3. Wildlife refuges

- TR's accomplishments in conservation
  - established 18 national monuments (like Grand Canyon)
  - created five national parks
  - designated 51 wildlife refuges
  - added 150 million acres of woods to forest reserves

- TR led an active life—
  - liked hiking and camping
  - lived in the West, drove cattle
  - went on African safari

- Before becoming president, served in Spanish-American War: Rough Riders

- Earned 1906 Nobel Peace Prize for ending Russo-Japanese War

- Set up the U.S. Forest Service in 1905

- Governor of NY 1899–1901

- Acquired the Panama Canal Zone in 1903

- President 1901–1909

- 26th president; born 1858; died 1919

- First conservation president

- Youngest president in history: age 42

- Foreign policy: "Speak softly and carry a big stick."

Prewriting

Organize

Use my notes to make a support pattern.

Now it's time for you to practice this strategy. Write the facts from page 54 under the appropriate main points. Use another sheet of paper, if you need more room.

Topic: Teddy Roosevelt

Main Point: Basic facts about his presidency and personal life

Supporting facts

_____

_____

_____

Main Point: Role in conservation

Supporting facts

_____

_____

_____

_____

Main Point: Other high points of presidency

Supporting facts

_____

_____

 You may wish to organize your notes on another topic on a separate sheet of paper.

 Now go back to Selena's work on page 112 in the Student Edition.

Drafting

Write
Draft the body of my report. Write a paragraph for each main point on my organizer.

your own writing

Now it's time for you to practice this strategy. On this page, you are going to write one or two paragraphs for the research report on Teddy Roosevelt or on your own topic. Choose one main point from the previous page or your own notes. Then use most or all of the facts you listed under that point in a paragraph or two.

_____

_____

_____

_____

_____

_____

_____

_____

_____

_____

_____

_____

_____

 Now go back to Selena's work on page 114 in the Student Edition.

Revising

Elaborate

Complete my report by adding an introduction and a conclusion.

Now it's time for you to practice this strategy. Read the two introductions below. Decide which one is better and explain why you think so on the lines. (You may see some errors.)

1. Theodore Roosevelt became president in 1901. He was the first conservation president. Before him, people did not care much about the environment. He made them more aware of the need to conserve our natural resources.

2. When Theodore Roosevelt became president of the United States in 1901, he brought his love of nature and the outdoors. He enjoyed hiking and camping and had lived in the West. Roosevelt realized that America was in danger of using up its resources, and he vowed to do something about it.

_____

_____

_____

Now read these two conclusions. Choose the better one and explain why you made that choice below. (You may see some errors.)

1. After Theodore Roosevelt left office, the movement to preserve natural resources continued. Today, Americans can hike, camp, boat, see wild animals, and breathe clean air in our National Parks and Refuges. Thanks to roosevelt and the people who continue his work, Earth's natural resources are being preserved and enjoyed.

2. Theodore Roosevelt's term ended in 1909. Fortunately, his work on the environment continued after that. He ran for president in 1912 but was defeated. He died in 1919.

_____

_____

_____

Remember: Use this strategy in **your own writing**

RETURN Now go back to Selena's work on page 115 in the Student Edition.

ReVising

Clarify

Delete any unnecessary information.

Now it's time for you to practice this strategy. Here is a paragraph from one writer's research report about Theodore Roosevelt. Read the paragraph and cross out any unnecessary information.

Theodore Roosevelt promised the American people that he would work on three important issues related to natural resources. He also told them about the time he spent in the Badlands of the Dakotas. The first issue was water. Roosevelt had traveled throughout the western United States, and he understood how streams and rivers could be used to irrigate dry areas. He explained how much he had enjoyed bird watching in the West. He knew that storing water could make it possible for more people to live in the West. He thought the East was getting too crowded. Roosevelt's second issue was forests. He wanted to make sure that the U.S. government managed woodlands responsibly so the forests would be preserved. His third issue was wildlife. Roosevelt knew that many plants and animals were dying out in the United States. He wanted to create wildlife preserves where plants and animals could live and grow.

Explain why the information you crossed out is unnecessary.

_____

_____

_____

_____

_____

_____

Remember: Use this strategy in **your own writing**

 Now go back to Selena's work on page 116 in the Student Edition.

Expository Writing • Research Report

Editing

Proofread

Check to see that I have capitalized words correctly.

Proofreading marks:
- ⌐ Indent.
- ≡ Make a capital.
- / Make a small letter.
- ∧ Add something.
- ℓ Take out something.
- ⊙ Add a period.
- ⌗ New paragraph
- ⟨SP⟩ Spelling error

Now it's time for you to practice this strategy. Here is part of the revised draft of the report about Theodore Roosevelt. Use the proofreading marks to correct any errors. Use a dictionary to help with spelling.

Some of the greatest acomplishments of Theodore Roosevelt's presidency were related to Conservation. He protected 150 million acres of woods by adding them to the u.s. forest preserves. He turned 18 places, including the grand canyon, into national monuments. He established five national parks and more than fifty wildlife refuges. Roosevelt did not do these things for political reasons. He really believed that Conservation was important. He wanted future generations of americans to be able to use and enjoy these natural resources.

After Theodore Roosevelt left office, the movement to preserve natural resources continued. Today, Americans can hike, camp, boat, see wild animals, and breathe clean air in our National Parks and Refuges. in fact, countries all over the world are now working to protect the water, air, oceans, and land. Thanks to roosevelt and the people who continue his work, Earth's natural resources are being preserved and enjoyed.

Remember: Use this strategy in **your own writing**

 RETURN

Now go back to Selena's work on page 118 in the Student Edition.

Expository Writing • Research Report

Using a Rubric

Use this rubric to evaluate Selena's report on pages 119–121 in your Student Edition. You may work with a partner.

Audience

Does the writer explain words that the audience might not understand?

Organization

Does the writer organize the body of the report so it clearly presents and develops the main points?

Elaboration

Do the introduction and conclusion add to the report by stating the topic and summarizing the main points?

Clarification

Does the writer focus the report by including only necessary information?

your own writing

Save this rubric. Use it to check your own writing.

Conventions & Skills

Does the writer correctly capitalize proper nouns, proper adjectives, and abbreviations?

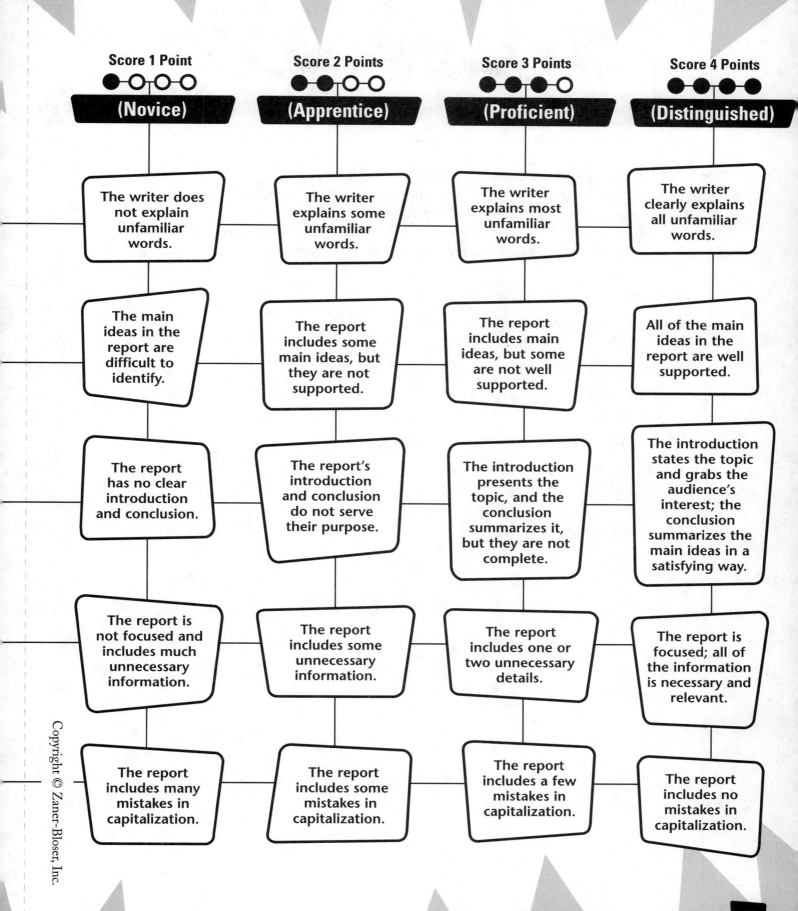

Score 1 Point
● ─ ○ ─ ○ ─ ○
(Novice)

Score 2 Points
● ─ ● ─ ○ ─ ○
(Apprentice)

Score 3 Points
● ─ ● ─ ● ─ ○
(Proficient)

Score 4 Points
● ─ ● ─ ● ─ ●
(Distinguished)

The writer does not explain unfamiliar words.

The writer explains some unfamiliar words.

The writer explains most unfamiliar words.

The writer clearly explains all unfamiliar words.

The main ideas in the report are difficult to identify.

The report includes some main ideas, but they are not supported.

The report includes main ideas, but some are not well supported.

All of the main ideas in the report are well supported.

The report has no clear introduction and conclusion.

The report's introduction and conclusion do not serve their purpose.

The introduction presents the topic, and the conclusion summarizes it, but they are not complete.

The introduction states the topic and grabs the audience's interest; the conclusion summarizes the main ideas in a satisfying way.

The report is not focused and includes much unnecessary information.

The report includes some unnecessary information.

The report includes one or two unnecessary details.

The report is focused; all of the information is necessary and relevant.

The report includes many mistakes in capitalization.

The report includes some mistakes in capitalization.

The report includes a few mistakes in capitalization.

The report includes no mistakes in capitalization.

Prewriting

Gather   Interview others and take notes.

Now it's your turn to practice this strategy with a different topic.
Suppose you are writing a compare-and-contrast essay about mysteries on TV and mysteries on the radio. You plan to interview Angela Murphy, a writer for Radio Mystery Theater. Put a star in front of each question that should help you gather good information for your essay.

_____ How long is a radio mystery?

_____ What kind of radio do you have?

_____ How important is imagination when you're creating a radio mystery?

_____ How do you make the sound effects for a radio mystery?

_____ What is your favorite sport?

_____ Where do you get the stories you make into radio mysteries?

_____ How is listening to a mystery different from watching one?

your own writing

Now write two questions you would like to ask Angela Murphy. Choose questions that will help you gather interesting information for your essay.

_____

_____

_____

_____

Prewriting

Gather
Interview others and take notes.

Here are the answers one writer received when he asked Angela Murphy two of the questions on page 62. The writer tape-recorded her answers so he would remember them. Read the answers and think about what information you will use in your essay. You will make notes on the next page.

Q: How important is imagination when you're creating a radio mystery?

A: Imagination is very important. Suppose you have a story and you want to make it into a radio show. When you read the story, you have to imagine that you're hearing it. Imagine what a scream sounds like. Imagine what a slamming door sounds like.

It's fun to put the sounds in. Sometimes I read a story out loud to myself and do the sound effects as I go along. It helps me plan what the audience will hear—and what the audience needs to hear. I have to remember that I can't show them anything. I have to present every clue with sound.

Q: How do you make the sound effects for a radio mystery?

A: Making sound effects can be so much fun. In the old days, there was at least one sound person on a radio show. He or she would use things like squeaky hinges, buckets of water, coconut shells, and people's voices to create the sound effects.

Today most of our sounds are already recorded. We just play them when and where we need them. Television and movies use recorded sound, too. Sometimes we get to be more creative. I always enjoy looking for new sounds to make and use.

Remember:
Use this strategy in **your own writing**

Now go back to Henry's work on page 131 in the Student Edition.

Copyright © Zaner-Bloser, Inc.

Prewriting

Organize

Organize my interview notes into an attribute chart. Include my own ideas, too.

your own writing

Now it's time for you to practice this strategy. Review the questions and answers on page 63. Organize that information into this attribute chart. Add your own ideas, too.

TV Mystery	Attribute	Radio Mystery
	What You See	
	What You Hear	
	Source of Clues	

RETURN

Now go back to Henry's work on page 132 in the Student Edition.

Write

Draft my essay. Discuss the likenesses and differences in separate paragraphs.

your own writing

Now it's time for you to practice this strategy. Review your notes and the chart on page 64. Then write a paragraph telling how TV mysteries and radio mysteries are alike. You can add your own ideas, too. Then read the directions on the next page.

_____

_____

_____

_____

_____

_____

_____

_____

_____

_____

_____

_____

_____

_____

_____

_____

_____

Drafting

Write
Draft my essay. Discuss the likenesses and differences in separate paragraphs.

your own writing

Now it's time for you to practice this strategy. This time, draft a paragraph about how TV and radio mysteries are different. Don't forget to include your own ideas.

_____

_____

_____

_____

_____

_____

_____

_____

_____

_____

_____

_____

_____

_____

_____

 Now go back to Henry's work on page 134 in the Student Edition.

ReVising

Elaborate

Make sure the information
I add helps to develop an
unbiased presentation.

Now it's time for you to practice this strategy. Read these sentences from
another writer's essay comparing television and radio mysteries. Put a star
next to the ones that are biased or unfair. Then rewrite those sentences to
make them unbiased.

_____ Television offers one way to tell a story. Radio offers a much
better way.

_____

_____

_____

_____ Radio relies on dialogue and sound effects to tell a story.
Television uses sights as well as sounds to tell a story.

_____

_____

_____

_____ Many people enjoy mysteries. Millions of people watch them on
TV every week. Radio mysteries also have a large audience,
but those people are smarter and have more imagination.

_____

_____

_____

Remember:
Use this strategy in
**your own
writing**

Now go back to Henry's work on page 135 in the Student Edition.

ReVising

Clarify

Rewrite stringy sentences to make them clearer.

Now it's time for you to practice this strategy. The sentences below are long and stringy. Rewrite them so that each sentence contains one clear idea.

1. If you're a fan of mysteries, you might want to tune in to Radio Mystery Theater some weeknight at 8:00 P.M. if you check your local listings to find out which station in your area plays it.

_____

_____

_____

_____

2. We put on a radio show at our school once and we played recordings that we made of a creaky door at Carl's house and drumsticks tapping on a tabletop sounded like a clock ticking really loud and Shari played a note on her electronic keyboard to make a doorbell sound.

_____

_____

_____

_____

_____

Remember: Use this strategy in **your own writing**

RETURN Now go back to Henry's work on page 136 in the Student Edition.

Expository Writing • Compare-and-Contrast Essay

⅃	Indent.	ℓ	Take out something.
≡	Make a capital.	⊙	Add a period.
/	Make a small letter.	#	New paragraph
∧	Add something.	SP	Spelling error

Editing

Proofread

Check to see that all titles are capitalized and punctuated correctly.

Now it's time for you to practice this strategy. Here is part of an essay about mysteries on TV and on the radio. Use the proofreading marks to correct any errors you find. Use a dictionary to help with spelling.

Mysteries often have interesting titles. A television mystery series for kids is named Are You Afraid Of The Dark? The title warns you that something scary is going to happen. What do you think a story called The tell-Tale Heart could be about? It is a famous story by Edgar Allan Poe that has been on television and on radio, to. Sometimes a title is the name of the main character, like the old television series Columbo and magnum, P.I.

Mysteries on the radio must have interesting titles, too. Two popular series were called The adventures of Sam Spade and "danger with Granger." One series was called I love a mystery. Your grandparents might have listened to a series of radio shows called The thin man. There was also a television series called "The thin man."

Remember: Use this strategy in **your own writing**

Now go back to Henry's work on page 138 in the Student Edition.

Using a Rubric

Use this rubric to evaluate Henry's essay on page 139 of your Student Edition. You can work with a partner.

Audience

How effectively does the writer get the reader's attention?

Organization

How clearly does the writer present likenesses and differences?

Elaboration

Does the writer include information that helps develop an unbiased (fair) presentation?

Clarification

Does the writer avoid using stringy, poorly constructed sentences?

Conventions & Skills

Does the writer capitalize and punctuate titles correctly?

your own writing

Save this rubric. Use it to check your own writing.

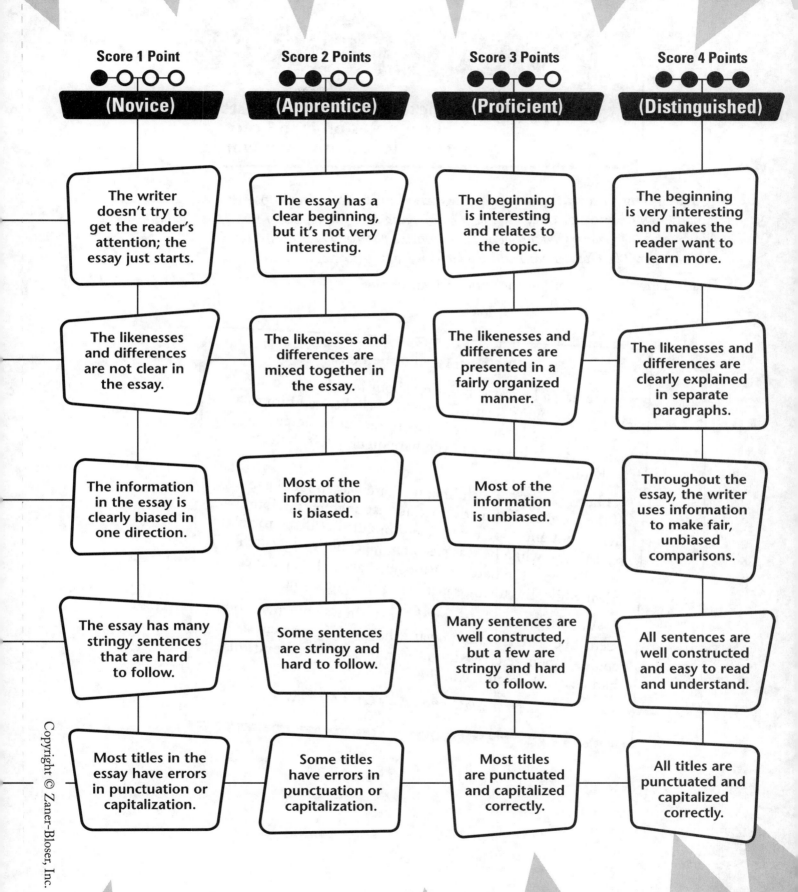

Score 1 Point ● ○ ○ ○ (Novice)

The writer doesn't try to get the reader's attention; the essay just starts.

The likenesses and differences are not clear in the essay.

The information in the essay is clearly biased in one direction.

The essay has many stringy sentences that are hard to follow.

Most titles in the essay have errors in punctuation or capitalization.

Score 2 Points ● ● ○ ○ (Apprentice)

The essay has a clear beginning, but it's not very interesting.

The likenesses and differences are mixed together in the essay.

Most of the information is biased.

Some sentences are stringy and hard to follow.

Some titles have errors in punctuation or capitalization.

Score 3 Points ● ● ● ○ (Proficient)

The beginning is interesting and relates to the topic.

The likenesses and differences are presented in a fairly organized manner.

Most of the information is unbiased.

Many sentences are well constructed, but a few are stringy and hard to follow.

Most titles are punctuated and capitalized correctly.

Score 4 Points ● ● ● ● (Distinguished)

The beginning is very interesting and makes the reader want to learn more.

The likenesses and differences are clearly explained in separate paragraphs.

Throughout the essay, the writer uses information to make fair, unbiased comparisons.

All sentences are well constructed and easy to read and understand.

All titles are punctuated and capitalized correctly.

Prewriting

Gather

Pick a fable that interests me.
Take notes on it so I can
rewrite it in my own words.

You are going to rewrite one of your favorite fables. You can choose the fable below or another one, such as *The Fox and the Grapes, The Town Mouse and the Country Mouse, The Lion and the Mouse, The Ants and the Grasshopper, The Goose That Laid the Golden Eggs,* or others.

Read the fable below or another one of your choice.

The Tortoise and the Hare

One day, a hare was boasting about how fast he could run. To the hare's surprise, a tortoise challenged him to a race. The hare laughed at the tortoise, but he agreed to race. The race began, and the hare quickly left the tortoise far behind.

Halfway to the finish line, the hare was so far ahead of the tortoise that he decided to rest a while. He found a shady spot and took a nap. He thought that if the tortoise passed him while he was sleeping, he could easily catch up. However, the hare slept longer than he had planned. Meanwhile, the tortoise just kept plodding along.

When the hare woke up, the tortoise was nowhere to be seen. The hare sprinted toward the finish line as fast as he could. When he arrived, however, he saw that the tortoise had beaten him and won the race.

Moral: Slow and steady wins the race.

Prewriting

Gather

Pick a fable that interests me. Take notes on it so I can rewrite it in my own words.

your own writing

Now it's your turn to practice this strategy. After you have chosen and read a fable, use this page to make notes on the plot events, the characters, and the moral. You can also use this space to brainstorm ways to make small changes in the fable and rewrite it in your own words. You do need to change the fable in some way, not just retell the same story.

_____

_____

_____

_____

_____

_____

_____

_____

_____

_____

_____

_____

_____

_____

_____

_____

 Now go back to Brian's work on page 151 in the Student Edition.

Prewriting

Organize

Organize the plot events using a cause-and-effect chain.

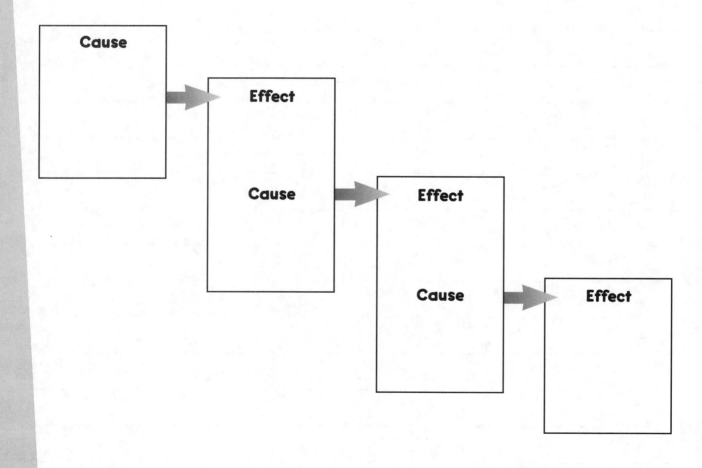

your own writing

Now it's time for you to practice this strategy. Use the cause-and-effect chain on this page to organize your notes from page 73. Write the first plot event in the first box. Write an effect in the second box, and then add another cause to the same box. Continue adding causes and effects until you have organized all the plot events in the fable. Add more boxes to the cause-and-effect chain, if necessary.

Cause

Effect

Cause

Effect

Cause

Effect

RETURN Now go back to Brian's work on page 152 in the Student Edition.

Drafting

Write

Draft my retelling of the fable. Make sure the causes and effects are clear.

your own writing

Now it's time for you to practice this strategy. Use the space on this page and the next page to draft your fable. Follow the pattern in your cause-and-effect chain. Make sure that your draft uses animals or objects as characters and has a moral.

_____

_____

_____

_____

_____

_____

_____

_____

_____

_____

_____

_____

_____

_____

_____

_____

_____

_____

Drafting

Write

Draft my retelling of the fable.
Make sure the causes and effects
are clear.

**your own
writing**   Use this space to write the rest of your fable.

_____

_____

_____

_____

_____

_____

_____

_____

_____

_____

_____

_____

_____

_____

 Now go back to Brian's work on page 154 in the Student Edition.

Revising

Elaborate
Add dialogue to make the story and characters come alive.

Now it's time for you to practice this strategy. Read these sentences from a retelling of *The Tortoise and the Hare.* Each sentence describes what a character says but does not contain dialogue. Rewrite the sentence so it contains dialogue.

1. One day, a swift hare was bragging about how fast he could run and how slow the tortoise was.

_____

_____

_____

2. After listening to the hare's boasting, the tortoise challenged him to a race.

_____

_____

_____

3. The hare said with a laugh that he was quite surprised at the tortoise's challenge.

_____

_____

_____

4. The hare thought the whole thing was a big joke, but he agreed to race the tortoise.

_____

_____

_____

Remember: Use this strategy in *your own writing*

 Now go back to Brian's work on page 155 in the Student Edition.

ReVising

Clarify

Make sure that all the plot events lead to the moral of the fable.

Now it's time for you to practice this strategy. Read this paragraph from another writer's retelling of *The Tortoise and the Hare*. The moral of the fable is "Slow and steady wins the race." Cross out any plot events that do not lead to this moral.

With all the other animals watching and cheering, the race began. To nobody's surprise, the hare took off like a shot. He had learned to run fast from his mother. The tortoise crawled along after him. Within a few minutes, the hare was so far ahead that he started to slow down. Then he happened to glance into a store window as he was passing. There, he saw the most incredible large-screen TV he had ever seen. It was on sale! Because he was so far ahead, he decided to go into the store and have a look at the TV. The hare had always wanted a large-screen TV because he was fond of watching nature specials and golf on television.

Remember: Use this strategy in **your own writing**

RETURN
Now go back to Brian's work on page 156 in the Student Edition.

Narrative Writing • Fable

Editing

Proofread

Check to see that I have not used double negatives.

⌐ Indent.	ℓ Take out something.
≡ Make a capital.	⊙ Add a period.
/ Make a small letter.	⌗ New paragraph
∧ Add something.	SP Spelling error

Now it's time for you to practice this strategy. This is the first part of one writer's retelling of *The Tortoise and the Hare*. Use the proofreading marks to correct any errors, especially double negatives. Use a dictionary to help with spelling.

The Tortoise and the Hare

One day, all the animals were gathered together in the forest. A swift hare braged, "I'm the fastest runner in the forest, and you, Tortoise, are without a doubt the slowest. You could not never beat me in a race!"

The tortoise listened to the hare's boasting, but he was very tired of it. He did not say nothing. He pulled his head back into his shell, but he could still hear the hare bragging.

When he could not stand it no longer, the tortoise answered, "Why don't we race, just to make sure you know what you're talking about?"

The hare's eyes bugged out, and he said with a laugh, "I'm really surprised that you are challenging me to a race! of course, the whole idea is one huge joke, but if you want to make a fool of yourself, I'll race you."

Remember: Use this strategy in **your own writing**

RETURN Now go back to Brian's work on page 158 in the Student Edition

Using a Rubric

Use this rubric to evaluate Brian's fable on pages 159–161 in your Student Edition. You may work with a partner.

Use this rubric to evaluate Brian's fable on pages 159–161 in your Student Edition.

Audience

Is the story interesting? Is the moral of the story clear to the reader?

Organization

Does the writer clearly indicate the causes and effects of plot events?

Elaboration

Does the writer use dialogue to make the story and characters come alive?

Clarification

Do all the plot events lead to the moral of the story?

Conventions & Skills

Does the writer avoid using double negatives?

your own writing

Save this rubric. Use it to check your own writing.

Score 1 Point ●○○○ (Novice)

Score 2 Points ●●○○ (Apprentice)

Score 3 Points ●●●○ (Proficient)

Score 4 Points ●●●● (Distinguished)

(Novice)	(Apprentice)	(Proficient)	(Distinguished)
The story is not very interesting and does not seem to have a moral.	The story is somewhat interesting. A moral is suggested but not clearly indicated.	The story holds the reader's attention. The moral is somewhat clear.	The story is very interesting, and the moral is very clear.
The causes and effects of plot events are not clear.	Some causes and effects are clear, but most are not.	Most causes and effects are clear.	All causes and effects are clear and well connected.
There is little or no dialogue.	There is some dialogue, but it is not interesting.	The dialogue is mostly interesting.	The dialogue is very interesting and makes the story and characters come alive.
Many of the plot events are not related to the moral of the story.	Several plot events are not related to the moral.	A few plot events are not related to the moral.	All of the plot events lead to the moral of the story.
The story contains many double negatives.	The story contains several double negatives.	The story contains a few double negatives.	The story contains no double negatives.

PrewRitiNg

Gather
Brainstorm some people and events for my mystery.

Here's how one writer got ready to write a mystery. She started by listing people and events her mystery could be about. Then she circled the one that interested her most: a lost homework assignment. Read what she wrote below.

People and Events My Mystery Could Be About

- The county fair: A stranger enters an animal in a contest at the fair, but he keeps the animal out of sight.

- A lost homework assignment: The assignment is done, but it disappears overnight.

- My great aunt Tilda: She has disappeared!

- A strange smell in the air: The air at school suddenly smells like peaches.

- An old box in the basement: A clear, sticky liquid is leaking out of one corner.

- Our new neighbor: Why does she seem to be hiding from us?

- A new teacher: What does she carry back and forth to school in that long, narrow box?

- A neighbor who disappears: He used to wave at me every morning, but now his house is dark and looks deserted.

- A new pet that does something strange: It might be a parrot that seems to be telling me something in a language I don't understand.

Prewriting

Gather
Brainstorm some people and events for my mystery.

your own writing

Now it's your turn to practice this strategy with a different topic. Start by listing several people and events that your mystery could be about. Then choose the one that interests you most and circle it.

People and Events My Mystery Could Be About

_____

_____

_____

_____

_____

_____

_____

_____

_____

_____

_____

_____

_____

_____

_____

_____

_____

 Now go back to Tia's work on page 173 in the Student Edition.

Prewriting

Organize

Make a story map to plan my mystery.

On this page, you can see the story map for one writer's mystery about the missing homework. Read it and then use the boxes on the next page to make a story map for your mystery.

Setting:

Place: home of fifth grader, a fifth-grade classroom

Time: now

Main Characters: Josh, a fifth grader; his mom; Mr. Randolph, his teacher

---

Problem/Mystery: Josh's homework assignment is missing. He did it one evening, but it is gone the next morning.

Plot:

Event 1: One morning, Josh goes to put his homework in his backpack, but he can't find it.

Event 2: He tells his teacher that the assignment is missing. The teacher gives him another day to find it.

Event 3: Josh looks for clues to the mystery.

Outcome: Josh finally solves the puzzle and turns in his assignment.

Prewriting

Organize

Make a story map to plan my mystery.

your own writing

Now it's time to practice this strategy. Use the boxes on this page to make a story map for your mystery. Add more events to the story map, if needed.

Setting:

Place:

Time:

Main Characters:

Problem/Mystery:

Plot:

Event 1:

Event 2:

Event 3:

Outcome:

RETURN
Now go back to Tia's work on page 174 in the Student Edition.

Drafting

Write
Draft my mystery, using the story map and paying special attention to the clues.

your own writing

Now it's time for you to practice this strategy. Below, list the clues you want to use in your mystery. You might change the clues as you write, but your list will give you a good starting point. Be careful not to give too much away!

Clues I Want to Include in My Mystery

_____

_____

_____

_____

Now use the rest of this page and the next page to write the first draft of your mystery. Follow your story map and work in the clues you listed above.

_____

_____

_____

_____

_____

_____

_____

_____

Drafting

Write

Draft my mystery, using the story map and paying special attention to the clues.

_____

_____

_____

_____

_____

_____

_____

_____

_____

_____

_____

_____

_____

_____

_____

_____

RETURN Now go back to Tia's work on page 176 in the Student Edition.

Revising

Elaborate

Add suspenseful words.
Use a thesaurus to find
new words.

Now it's time for you to practice this strategy. Here are some sentences from one writer's mystery. Notice that some words are underlined. Use a thesaurus to find a more suspenseful and interesting word to replace each underlined word.

1. Josh was completely <u>confused</u> _____.

The folder with his homework had been sitting on the counter

when he went to bed last night. Now it had <u>disappeared</u>

_____!

2. As he walked into class, Josh was <u>worried</u> _____.

What would Mr. Randolph say about the missing assignment?

3. As Josh slowly pushed open the door of the barn, he heard a <u>sound</u>

_____. It took a while for his eyes to

adjust to the <u>black</u> _____ darkness.

4. His hand was <u>shaking</u> _____

as he reached toward the sleeping pig.

5. Quickly, he reached behind the pig and <u>took</u> _____

_____ the papers it had been lying on.

 Now go back to Tia's work on page 177 in the Student Edition.

Narrative Writing • Mystery

ReVising

Clarify   Check for conflicting information.

Now it's time for you to practice this strategy. Read the paragraph on this page. What conflicting information did you find? Explain the problem on the lines. Then revise the paragraph so the information in it does not conflict.

Josh ate his breakfast under a deep, dark cloud. The folder with his assignment was gone. It was as if one of the farm animals had come into the house last night and eaten his homework! Of course, he could make another copy of his report from his notes, but what about the illustrations he had drawn? It would take a week to redo them. He decided to skip breakfast and take one more look around the house.

The Problem:

_____

_____

_____

_____

_____

_____

_____

Remember:
Use this strategy in *your own writing*

Now go back to Tia's work on page 178 in the Student Edition.

Editing

Proofread

Check to see that I have punctuated quotations correctly.

Now it's time for you to practice this strategy. Proofread the end of this mystery about the missing homework. Correct any spelling, capitalization, and punctuation errors. Pay special attention to how the writer punctuated the quotations. Use a dictionary to help with spelling.

Josh was stunned. His mom had just told him that "she might have taken his homework assignment out to the barn, along with old newspapers." He had seen her take old newspapers out to the barn a hundred times. Their pig slept on straw and newspapers.

Josh had heard the old joke people told "about a dog eating somebody's homework." Had the pig ate his report? It couldn't be true!

As josh slowly pushed open the door of the barn, he heard a creak. It took a while for his eyes to ajust to the inky darknes. His hand was trembling as he reached toward the sleeping pig. Josh jumped when the huge pig gave "a groan and a grunt." Luckily, it did not wake up. Then the pig rolled over, and Josh saw his chance Quickly, he reached behind the pig and snatched the papers it had been lying on.

Editing

⅂ Indent.	ℓ Take out something.
≡ Make a capital.	⊙ Add a period.
/ Make a small letter.	⌗ New paragraph
∧ Add something.	SP Spelling error

Proofread

Check to see that I have punctuated quotations correctly.

His hart fell when he saw the papers were not his report.
They were an old newspaper and a sheet of corn prices. Oh,
no he cried, loud enough for the pig to wake up.

Josh stumbled backward, bumping against a feeder on the
pen wall. His hand went into the feeder, which was half-filled
with hay. then he felt something that definitly wasn't hay.
When he pulled it out, he couldn't believe his eyes. Hooray he
yelled. It was his Homework assignment!

Now he knew what had happened. His mom had brouhgt his
papers out to the barn by mistake, but they did not fall into
the pigs pen. They had dropped into the sheeps feeder! He
noticed that only a tiny corner of one page had been nibbled.
"Good sheep! Josh said to the woolly animal. He was never so
happy in his life that sheep eat only grass!

Remember: Use this strategy in **your own writing**

Now go back to Tia's work on page 180 in the Student Edition.

Using a Rubric

Use this rubric to evaluate Tia's mystery on pages 181–183 in your Student Edition. You may work with a partner.

Audience

Has the writer chosen characters and a plot that appeal to the audience?

Organization

Does the story contain clues for the characters and the reader?

Elaboration

Does the writer use suspenseful words to create a feeling of mystery?

Clarification

Does all the information in the story make sense?

Conventions & Skills

Are quotations punctuated correctly?

your own writing

Save this rubric. Use it to check your own writing.

Score 1 Point ●○○○ (Novice)	Score 2 Points ●●○○ (Apprentice)	Score 3 Points ●●●○ (Proficient)	Score 4 Points ●●●● (Distinguished)
The characters and plot are not very appealing.	The characters and plot have some appeal.	The characters and plot are fairly appealing.	The characters and plot are very appealing.
The story contains few clues, and they are hard to follow.	Some clues are helpful, but most are difficult to follow.	Most of the clues are helpful.	All clues are helpful and clever, and they add to the story.
The story contains few suspenseful words.	The story contains some suspenseful words.	The story contains several suspenseful words.	The story contains many suspenseful words.
The story contains many conflicting details and events.	The story contains several conflicting details and events.	The story contains a few conflicting details and events.	The story contains no conflicting details or events.
Few of the quotes are punctuated correctly.	Some quotes are punctuated correctly.	Most quotes are punctuated correctly.	All quotes are punctuated correctly.

PreWRiting

Gather

As I read my book, take notes on ideas I might include in my review.

Read these notes that a writer took as she read *Terrible Things* by Eve Bunting.

Notes About Terrible Things
by Eve Bunting

- According to the cover, the story is an **allegory**, or retelling, of the Holocaust.

- Different animals live peacefully in a forest.

- One day, the Terrible Things come and take away "every creature with feathers."

- The Terrible Things represent the Nazis.

- After the birds are taken, the other animals feel relieved they were not captured.

- The main character is Little Rabbit, who asks the other animals why the birds were taken. However, the other animals don't want to think about what happened.

- Soon the Terrible Things come back for more animals (creatures with bushy tails, creatures that swim, creatures that sprout quills).

- Finally, the Terrible Things come for white creatures.

- All the rabbits are taken except Little Rabbit, who hides. As the story ends, he goes off to warn creatures in other parts of the forest.

- The story ends with this question: "If we had stuck together, would things have turned out differently?"

PreWriting

Gather

As I read my book, take notes on ideas I might include in my review.

your own writing

Now it's your turn to practice this strategy with a different topic. Choose a book to review and use this page to take notes on it. You will use these notes to organize and draft your own book review.

Notes on _____ by _____

_____

_____

_____

_____

_____

_____

_____

_____

_____

_____

_____

_____

RETURN Now go back to Jared's work on page 195 in the Student Edition.

PreWriting

Organize

Use my notes to make a pros-and-cons chart.

Below is a pros-and-cons chart that one writer made using the notes on *Terrible Things* on page 94. Notice how the writer has organized the notes into categories, such as plot, theme, and setting.

	Pros (what I liked)	Cons (what I disliked)
Plot	The story echoed the events of the Holocaust.	
Theme	The message is that we must all stick together if we want to defeat evil.	
Setting		The setting wasn't very well described; it's just a forest.
Characters	The Terrible Things were spooky. It was good that the author didn't describe them very much. They remain mysterious and frightening.	Little Rabbit was kind of blah.
Language	The animals make excuses and try not to think about what is happening— just like some people do when bad things happen.	
Other	It seemed almost like a fable with talking animal characters, but it explains how some people living in Nazi Germany must have felt.	

PreWriting

Organize Use my notes to make a pros-and-cons chart.

your own writing

Now it's time for you to practice this strategy. Use the blank chart on this page to make a pros-and-cons chart for your own book review. This chart will help you decide what you like and dislike about the book and organize your review of it.

Title of book: _____

Author: _____

	Pros (what I liked)	Cons (what I disliked)
Plot		
Theme		
Setting		
Characters		
Language		
Other		

RETURN

Now go back to Jared's work on page 196 in the Student Edition.

Drafting

Write Draft my book review, starting with my thesis statement.

Now it's time for you to practice this strategy. Here is the opening paragraph from a review of *Terrible Things*. Find and underline the writer's thesis statement.

In Terrible Things, Eve Bunting creates an allegory, or retelling, of the events of the Holocaust. Everyone should read this thought-provoking book. Using animals, the author helps readers better understand the thoughts and feelings of those caught in a terrible situation. The characters represent the people living in Germany in the 1930s. They are forest animals, including rabbits, birds, and fish. The evil Terrible Things in the story represent the Nazis.

your own writing Now write the opening paragraph of your own book review. Include a thesis statement that expresses your opinion of the book.

_____

_____

_____

_____

_____

_____

RETURN Now go back to Jared's work on page 198 in the Student Edition.

Revising

Elaborate

Include quotations and examples to support my opinion.

Now it's time for you to practice this strategy. Here is part of the book review of *Terrible Things.* Place a check mark where the author could have included a quotation or example to support her opinion. Then explain why you think a quotation or example is needed at that particular place.

Bunting's use of language is especially effective when different animals make excuses. In other parts of the book, she often repeats words to strengthen the feeling of approaching evil.

_____

_____

_____

_____

_____

_____

_____

_____

_____

_____

Remember: Use this strategy in **your own writing**

RETURN Now go back to Jared's work on page 199 in the Student Edition.

Copyright © Zaner-Bloser, Inc.

ReVising

Clarify

Restate my opinion at the end of the book review.

Now it's time for you to practice this strategy. Here are three possible paragraphs to end the review of *Terrible Things*. Read them and decide which one you would use. Then explain why each paragraph should—or should not—end the review. You might begin by rereading the author's opening paragraph on page 98.

Paragraph 1

The setting of the book is a forest clearing. Here, the animals have lived in peace for a long time. As Bunting writes, "They were content. Until the day the Terrible Things came." The setting is not well described in the book, although the drawings show it.

Paragraph 2

Bunting's language, plot, and characters create a powerful story that most readers will enjoy. The theme is clear: only by uniting and working together can the forest creatures—as well as we human beings—defeat the evil around us. As Little Rabbit explains, "I should have tried to help the other rabbits. If only we creatures had stuck together, it could have been different."

Paragraph 3

Bunting's book is interesting and well written but somewhat depressing. Most readers would probably enjoy one of her other books more, such as *Riding the Tiger*. That book is about a boy who finds out that it's easier to get on a tiger than to get off.

_____

_____

_____

_____

_____

_____

Remember: Use this strategy in **your own writing**

RETURN Now go back to Jared's work on page 200 in the Student Edition.

Editing

Proofread

Make sure pronoun antecedents are clear. Check to see that pronouns agree with their antecedents in number.

Indent.
Make a capital.
Make a small letter.
Add something.
Take out something.
Add a period.
New paragraph
(SP) Spelling error

Now it's time for you to practice this strategy. Here is part of the book review of *Terrible Things*. Use the proofreading marks to correct any errors. Use a dictionary to help with spelling.

The plot of the book echoes the events of the Holocast in Nazi Germany, when Jews and other people were arrested. He were taken to concentration camps and later killed. Like most people in Germany, the forrest creatures at first cannot believe what is happening to him. They try to convince themselves that the evil will be limited to others and that she will be safe. However, he soon learns that no one is safe from the Terrible Things.

The book's theme is stated at the end. Little Rabbit says that if the animals had all stuck together and supported each other in the face of danger, he might have been able to save himself. Little Rabbit manages to save himself by hidding behind a rock.

Remember:
Use this strategy in
your own writing

RETURN Now go back to Jared's work on page 202 in the Student Edition.

Using a Rubric

Use this rubric to evaluate Jared's book review on pages 203–205 in your Student Edition. You may work with a partner.

Audience

Does the writer begin by clearly explaining his or her opinion to the audience?

Organization

Does the writer organize the review around the book's theme, characters, plot, and setting?

Elaboration

Does the writer include quotations and examples to support his or her opinion?

Clarification

Does the writer clearly restate his or her opinion at the end of the review?

your own writing

Save this rubric. Use it to check your own writing.

Conventions & Skills

Do all pronouns have clear antecedents? Do the pronouns agree with their antecedents in number?

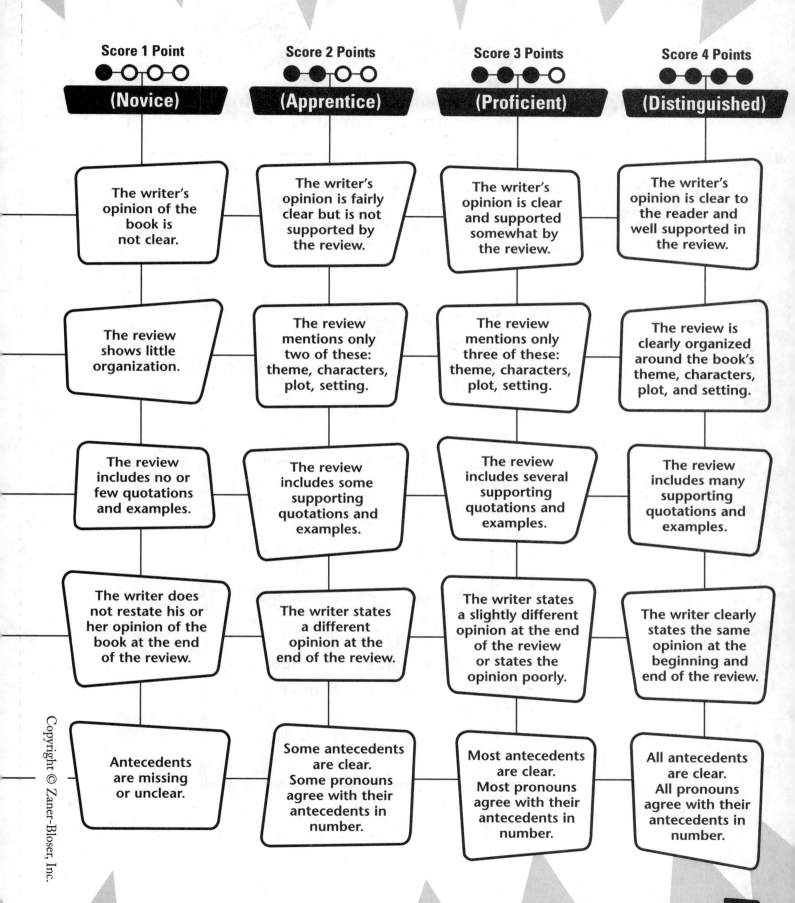

Score 1 Point

● ○ ○ ○

(Novice)

Score 2 Points

● ● ○ ○

(Apprentice)

Score 3 Points

● ● ● ○

(Proficient)

Score 4 Points

● ● ● ●

(Distinguished)

The writer's opinion of the book is not clear.	The writer's opinion is fairly clear but is not supported by the review.	The writer's opinion is clear and supported somewhat by the review.	The writer's opinion is clear to the reader and well supported in the review.
The review shows little organization.	The review mentions only two of these: theme, characters, plot, setting.	The review mentions only three of these: theme, characters, plot, setting.	The review is clearly organized around the book's theme, characters, plot, and setting.
The review includes no or few quotations and examples.	The review includes some supporting quotations and examples.	The review includes several supporting quotations and examples.	The review includes many supporting quotations and examples.
The writer does not restate his or her opinion of the book at the end of the review.	The writer states a different opinion at the end of the review.	The writer states a slightly different opinion at the end of the review or states the opinion poorly.	The writer clearly states the same opinion at the beginning and end of the review.
Antecedents are missing or unclear.	Some antecedents are clear. Some pronouns agree with their antecedents in number.	Most antecedents are clear. Most pronouns agree with their antecedents in number.	All antecedents are clear. All pronouns agree with their antecedents in number.

PrewRitiNg

Gather
Use what I read and learn from others to form an opinion about a topic.

Read these notes that one student made for a letter to the editor. The notes are based on his observations, plus interviews with other students and school staff. As you can tell, the writer has already gathered enough information to decide that the school grounds need help.

My Notes on the School Grounds

- Our school grounds are messy.
  - They have lots of litter, paper, pop bottles, and other trash.
  - Bike racks are tipped over.
  - Bushes need trimming.
  - The grounds need new flowers, plants, and trees.
  - The sports fields need to be cleaned and fixed up.
  - New paint is needed at several locations.

- Here is why we should clean up the school grounds:
  - We will enjoy coming to school more.
  - We will have more pride in our school.
  - Parents and other adults will have more respect for us.
  - We can build school spirit by working together.

PrewRitiNg

Gather

Use what I read and learn from others to form an opinion about a topic.

your own writing

Now it's your turn to practice this strategy with a different topic. Use this page to take notes on a topic or issue you feel strongly about. It could be an issue of concern in your school, community, or state. You will use these notes to organize and draft your own letter to the editor.

Notes on _____

- _____
  _____

- _____
  _____

- _____
  _____

- _____
  _____

- _____
  _____

- _____
  _____

- _____
  _____

RETURN

Now go back to Halle's work on page 215 in the Student Edition.

Prewriting

Organize
Make an outline to focus and support my opinion.

Below is part of a topic outline that a writer made using the notes on page 104. Read his notes.

I. Problems with the school grounds
- **A.** Litter and trash
- **B.** Bike racks tipped over
- **C.** Bushes overgrown and unhealthy
- **D.** New plantings needed
- **E.** Sports fields need cleaning
- **F.** New paint needed in many places

II. Benefits of making school grounds more attractive
- **A.** More pleasant to come to school
- **B.** Increased pride among students
- **C.** Increased respect from parents, other adults, and community members
- **D.** Increased school spirit from working together on a project

Now it's time for you to practice this strategy. You will help this writer organize each section of his letter. Decide which of the problems listed in the first section (I.) of his outline is most important. Write the letter of that problem (A.–F.) below and explain why you think it is the most important. Then decide which of the benefits (II.) is most important. Write its letter (A.–D.) and explain your choice.

Most Important Problem: _____

_____

_____

_____

Most Important Benefit: _____

_____

_____

_____

Prewriting

Organize
Make an outline to focus and support my opinion.

your own writing

Now it's time for you to practice this strategy. Make an outline below for your own letter to the editor. You can use a sentence outline or a topic outline. Use your notes on page 105. Outline only the reasons you will use to support your opinion. Put them in order from most important to least important. Use another sheet of paper if you need more room.

I. _____

   A. _____

   B. _____

   C. _____

II. _____

   A. _____

   B. _____

   C. _____

III. _____

   A. _____

   B. _____

   C. _____

RETURN

Now go back to Halle's work on page 216 in the Student Edition.

Write Draft my letter to the editor. State my opinion, support it, and sum up my argument.

your own writing

Now it's time for you to practice this strategy. On these two pages, draft your own letter to the editor, using your notes on page 105 and your outline on page 107. Start with your opinion, support it, and sum up your argument at the end of your letter. You do not need to include all the parts of a business letter, such as the heading and salutation, in this draft.

_____

_____

_____

_____

_____

_____

_____

_____

_____

_____

_____

_____

_____

Drafting

Write

Draft my letter to the editor. State my opinion, support it, and sum up my argument.

_____

_____

_____

_____

_____

_____

_____

_____

_____

_____

_____

_____

_____

_____

_____

_____

_____

_____

_____

_____

_____

Now go back to Halle's work on page 218 in the Student Edition.

ReVising

Elaborate   Add reasons and facts to support my opinion.

Now it's time for you to practice this strategy. Read this paragraph from a draft of a letter to the editor about the school grounds. Use the space below to write a note to this writer. Explain where he might add more reasons and facts. Describe the kinds of reasons and facts he might include. Refer to this writer's notes and outline on pages 104 and 106. (You will see some errors in this paragraph, as this is his first draft.)

> Making the school grounds more attactive will have many benefits for our school and for the community. Because of these many benefits, I suggest we start a project to improve the ap^pearance of our school grounds. The work force could include current and former students, parents, and teachers. And any community member. I believe that the largest group should be students We are the ones who will benefit most from an attractive, clean, and safe school.

_____

_____

_____

_____

_____

_____

Remember: Use this strategy in **your own writing**

 Now go back to Halle's work on page 219 in the Student Edition.

Clarify   Add signal words to clarify my ideas.

Now it's time for you to practice this strategy. Signal words act like road signs. They show that the writer is making an important point, changing direction, or coming to the conclusion. Read the following paragraph from the draft of one writer's letter to the editor. Then insert signal words where they will help make the ideas clearer. Choose from the signal words in the box.

Signal Words

therefore	on the other hand
for this reason	but
in addition	in the same way
as a result	in fact
meanwhile	for example

Dear Editor:

   I am a student at Somerset elementary School. I am writing to address a

serious problem at our school. Our school grounds are unattractive. They

are littered with trash. The plantings are weedy and overgrown. New paint

and repairs are needed in many locations. People must think that we do

not care about our school. I know this is not true. It's time for us to get

buzy and make the school grounds a more beautiful place.

Now go back to Halle's work on page 220 in the Student Edition.

Remember: Use this strategy in your own writing

Persuasive Writing • Letter to the Editor

Editing

Indent.	Take out something.
Make a capital.	Add a period.
Make a small letter.	New paragraph
Add something.	Spelling error

Proofread

Check that I have written all six parts of a business letter correctly and that there are no sentence fragments.

Now it's time for you to practice this strategy. Proofread this letter, using the proofreading marks. Check to make sure the writer has not written any sentence fragments and has written all six parts of a business letter correctly. Use a dictionary to help with spelling.

4517 Cook street

Providence, RI 029—

March 12, 20—

Providence Tribune

470 West 8th Avenue

Providence, RI 029—

Dear Editor

   I am a student at Somerset elementary School. I am writing to address

a serious problem at our school. Our school grounds are unattractive. For

example, they are littered with trash. The plantings are weedy and over-

grown. In addition, new paint and repairs are needed in many locations.

As a result, people must think that we do not care about our school. In

fact, I know this is not true. It's time for us to get buzy and make the

school grounds a more beautiful place.

Editing

⅃ Indent.	ℒ Take out something.
≡ Make a capital.	⊙ Add a period.
/ Make a small letter.	♯ New paragraph
∧ Add something.	⑆ Spelling error

Proofread

Check that I have written all six parts of a business letter correctly and that there are no sentence fragments.

Making the school grounds more attactive will have many benefits for our school and for the community. Perhaps the most important benefit. Increased school spirit from working together on an importent project. Some other benefits is increased pride among students and increased respect for students from parents, other adults, and community members.

Because of these many benefits, I suggest we start a project to improve the appearance of our school grounds. The work force could include current and former students, parents, and teachers. And any community member. I believe, however, that the largest group should be students Why. We are the ones who will benefit most from an attractive, clean, and safe school. We are the ones who have the most to gain. Let's get started!

Cameron Edwards

Cameron Edwards

Remember: Use this strategy in **your own writing**

Now go back to Halle's work on page 222 in the Student Edition.

Using a Rubric

Use this rubric to evaluate Halle's letter to the editor on page 223 in your Student Edition. You may work with a partner.

Audience

Does the writer focus on a topic that will interest the readers?

Organization

Does the writer organize his or her reasons from most important to least important?

Elaboration

Does the writer support his or her opinions with reasons and facts?

Clarification

Does the writer use signal words to clarify his or her ideas?

your own writing

Save this rubric. Use it to check your own writing.

Conventions & Skills

Does the writer include all six parts of a business letter and avoid sentence fragments?

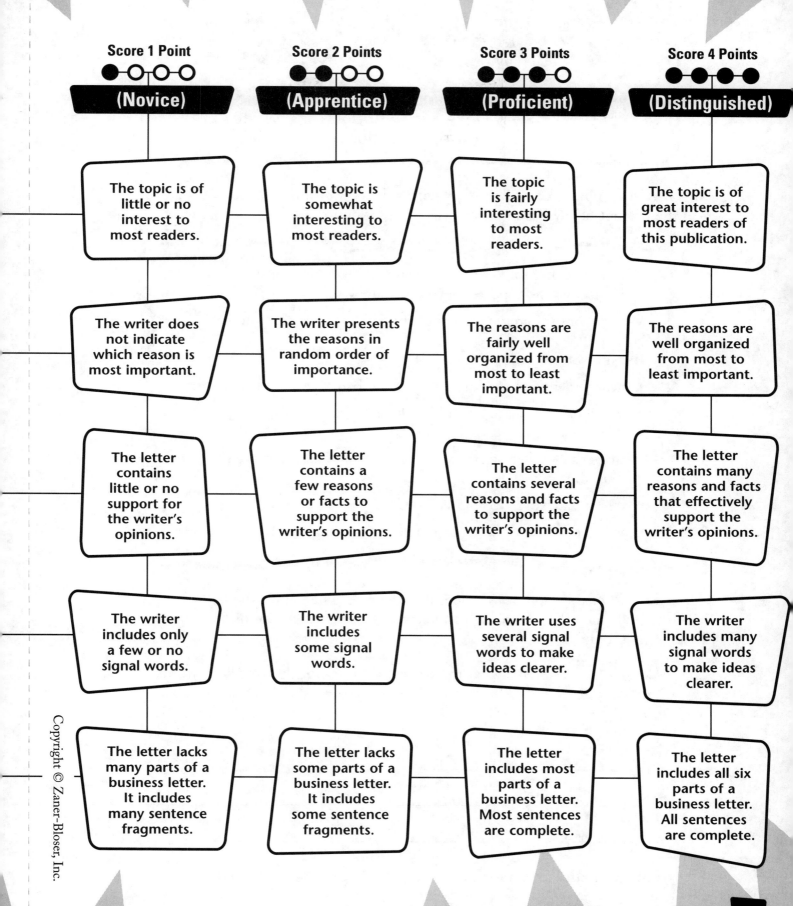

Score 1 Point ●━○━○━○ (Novice)	Score 2 Points ●━●━○━○ (Apprentice)	Score 3 Points ●━●━●━○ (Proficient)	Score 4 Points ●━●━●━● (Distinguished)
The topic is of little or no interest to most readers.	The topic is somewhat interesting to most readers.	The topic is fairly interesting to most readers.	The topic is of great interest to most readers of this publication.
The writer does not indicate which reason is most important.	The writer presents the reasons in random order of importance.	The reasons are fairly well organized from most to least important.	The reasons are well organized from most to least important.
The letter contains little or no support for the writer's opinions.	The letter contains a few reasons or facts to support the writer's opinions.	The letter contains several reasons and facts to support the writer's opinions.	The letter contains many reasons and facts that effectively support the writer's opinions.
The writer includes only a few or no signal words.	The writer includes some signal words.	The writer uses several signal words to make ideas clearer.	The writer includes many signal words to make ideas clearer.
The letter lacks many parts of a business letter. It includes many sentence fragments.	The letter lacks some parts of a business letter. It includes some sentence fragments.	The letter includes most parts of a business letter. Most sentences are complete.	The letter includes all six parts of a business letter. All sentences are complete.

PreWriting

Gather
Read and analyze the writing prompt. Make sure I understand what I am supposed to do.

Now it's time to practice this strategy with a different topic. Carefully read the prompt below. Think about what it asks you to do.

> You are packing for a long trip. You will take one item that is not really useful but is special to you in some way.
>
> Write about the item you would choose. Explain why you would choose it.
> Be sure your writing
>
> - clearly identifies the topic for your audience early in the paper.
> - is well organized. You should include an introduction, body, and conclusion.
> - includes details or facts that help readers understand each main idea.
> - uses signal words to connect ideas.
> - uses the conventions of language and spelling correctly.

Circle the part of the prompt that describes the task. Then circle the key word that tells the kind of writing you need to do. Draw a box around the Scoring Guide.

Describe what the test asks you to do. Use your own words.

_____

_____

_____

 Now go back to Phanna's work on page 236 in the Student Edition.

PreWriting
Gather & Organize

Choose a graphic organizer. Use it to organize my ideas.
Check my graphic organizer against the Scoring Guide.

Now it's time to practice these strategies. Go back and reread the writing prompt on page 116. Then fill in this network tree to plan your explanation of the object you would take with you. Add more circles and lines if you need them.

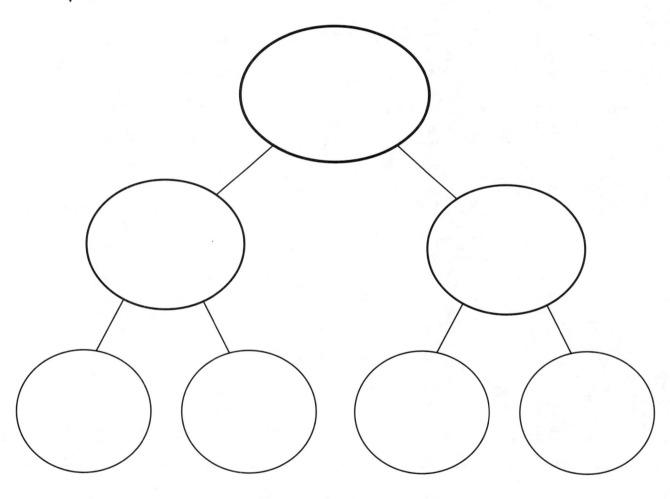

Now check your network tree against the Scoring Guide on page 116.
Make any changes that you think will improve your explanation.

 Now go back to Phanna's work on page 240 in the Student Edition.

Drafting

Write
Use my network tree to write an explanation with a good introduction, body, and conclusion.

your own writing

Now it's your turn to practice this strategy. Refer to your network tree on page 117 as you draft your explanation on this page and the next page. Include an introduction that clearly identifies your topic, a body that explains your reasons, and a conclusion that summarizes your main points.

_____

_____

_____

_____

_____

_____

_____

_____

_____

_____

_____

_____

_____

_____

Use after page 24I in the Student Edition.

Drafting

Write
Use my network tree to write an explanation with a good introduction, body, and conclusion.

_____

_____

_____

_____

_____

_____

_____

_____

_____

_____

_____

_____

_____

_____

_____

_____

RETURN

Now go back to Phanna's work on page 242 in the Student Edition.

ReVising

Elaborate

Check what I have written against the Scoring Guide. Add any missing facts or details.

Now it's time for you to practice this strategy. The paragraphs below are part of one student's draft response to the writing prompt on page 116. The student is explaining why he would pack a rabbit puppet. Rewrite the paragraphs. Add two or more sentences with details that tell who, what, when, where, or how. You can make up details if you wish.

> Their is something that's not really useful that I would pack, too. It's a silly old sock puppet named Jack.
>
> I enjoy playing with Jack sometimes, making him move like a real rabbit.

_____

_____

_____

_____

_____

_____

_____

Remember: Use this strategy in *your own writing*

 Now go back to Phanna's work on page 243 in the Student Edition.

Revising

Clarify

Check what I have written against the Scoring Guide. Make sure I have used signal words so that everything is clear.

Now it's time for you to practice this strategy. Decide where the signal words below belong in this draft. At each place where you see a ^, add signal words from the Word Bank that will help clarify and connect the ideas. This is a draft, so you will see some errors that you can correct now or later.

Word Bank

, but
because
As a finishing touch,

Next,
First,

Jack don't actually belong to me. I've been taking

care of him. Jack belongs to my big sister Pam. He is
                    ^

special partly because Pam made him. She got an old
                                        ^

sock and sewed on a couple of buttons for eyes. She
                                            ^

cut up an old bath towel to make his ears. She sewed
                                        ^

some pieces of fishing line to his nose to make whiskers.

You can bend his ears Pam put pipe cleaners inside them.
                    ^

Remember:
Use this strategy in
your own
writing

Now go back to Phanna's work on page 244 in the Student Edition.

Proofreading Marks	
⊐ Indent.	ℓ Take out something.
≡ Make a capital.	⊙ Add a period.
/ Make a small letter.	⌗ New paragraph
∧ Add something.	⑤⑨ Spelling error

Editing

Proofread
Check that I have used correct grammar, capitalization, punctuation, and spelling.

Now it's time for you to practice this strategy. Below is a revised explanation about the object one student would take on a trip. Use the proofreading marks to correct any errors in grammar, capitalization, punctuation, and spelling.

I'd Pack Jack
by Tracy Dobbins

If I went away from home, of course I'd pack clean socks and my toothbrush. Their is another item that's not really useful that I would pack, too. It's a silly old sock puppet named Jack. His full name is Jack rabbit.

Jack don't actually belong to me. I've been taking care of him. Jack really belongs to my big sister Pam. He is special partly because Pam made him. She got an old sock and sewed on a couple of buttons for eyes. She cut up an old bath towel to make his ears. She sewed some pieces of fishing line to his nose to make whiskers. You can bend his ears Pam put pipe cleaners inside them.

Me and Pam are really close, even though we are not nothing close in age. Pam is a soldier in the National guard. She's really far away from home right now. And I try to

Editing

Proofread

Check that I have used correct grammar, capitalization, punctuation, and spelling.

⊐ Indent.
≡ Make a capital.
/ Make a small letter.
∧ Add something.
℮ Take out something.
⊙ Add a period.
New paragraph
SP Spelling error

right to her a few times a week. Pam gave me Jack long before she joined the National Guard. After Pam made Jack for a school play, she said I could borrow him if I took really good care of him. She really meant I could have him.

Every time I get one of Pams letters, she asks how Jack is and reminds me to take good care of him. Somehow it seems that if I take good care of Jack, then Pam will be okay, too. I miss her I don't never worry about her so much if I hold Jack while I read her letters.

If I were taking a trip anywere in the world, I would pack Jack. Even though he might take up room for something more useful, I'd rather have Jack. He reminds me of my sister. Besides, I promized I would always be responsible for them.

Remember: Use this strategy in **your own writing**

RETURN Now go back to page 247 in the Student Edition.

Using a Rubric

This rubric for expository writing was developed from the Scoring Guide on page 227 in the Student Edition.

Audience

Does the writer clearly identify the topic for the audience early in the paper?

Organization

Is the paper well organized, including an introduction, body, and conclusion?

Elaboration

Does the writer include details or facts that help readers understand each main idea?

Clarification

Does the writer use signal words to connect ideas?

your own writing

Save this rubric. Use it to check your own writing.

Conventions & Skills

Does the writer use the conventions of language and spelling correctly?

Score 1 Point
(Novice)

The topic is not clear to the audience throughout the paper.

The paper rambles and is not organized into an introduction, body, and conclusion.

The paper includes few details or facts to support the main ideas.

The paper includes few signal words.

The paper has many errors in language use and spelling.

Score 2 Points
(Apprentice)

Several topics are mentioned, but it's not clear which is the main one.

The paper is missing the introduction and the conclusion.

The paper includes some details or facts.

The paper includes some signal words, but they are not used effectively.

The paper has several errors in language use and spelling.

Score 3 Points
(Proficient)

The topic is not clear until the end of the paper.

The paper is missing the introduction or the conclusion.

The paper includes many details or facts, but they are not always linked to main ideas.

The paper includes several signal words, but some are not used effectively.

The paper has a few errors in language use and spelling.

Score 4 Points
(Distinguished)

The topic is clearly identified for the audience at the beginning of the paper.

The paper is well organized into an introduction, body, and conclusion.

The paper includes many details or facts that help readers understand the main ideas.

The paper includes many signal words, and they are used effectively to connect ideas.

The paper has no errors in language use or spelling.